BISON
BOOKS

Christgau, John.
Michael and the whiz
kids : a story of baske
[2013]
33305229390558
cu   04/02/14

Michael
and the
Whiz Kids

A Story of Basketball,
Race, and Suburbia
in the 1960s

JOHN CHRISTGAU

University of Nebraska Press
Lincoln & London

© 2013 by the Board of Regents of the University of
Nebraska
All rights reserved
Manufactured in the United States of America

∞

Library of Congress Cataloging-in-Publication Data
Christgau, John.
Michael and the whiz kids: a story of basketball,
race, and suburbia in the 1960s / John Christgau.
pages cm
Includes bibliographical references.
ISBN 978-0-8032-4589-1 (pbk.: alk. paper)
ISBN 978-0-8032-4935-6 (epub)
ISBN 978-0-8032-4936-3 (mobi)
ISBN 978-0-8032-4844-1 (pdf)
1. Crestmoor High School (San Bruno, Calif.)—Bas-
ketball—History. 2. Crestmoor Falcons (Basketball
team)—History. 3. Basketball—Social aspects—Cali-
fornia. I. Title.
GV885.43.C74C47 2013
796.323'620979469—dc23   2013024702

Set in Sabon by Hannah Gokie.

Contents

Acknowledgments

Over a hundred people agreed to interviews with me so that I could re-create the story of Michael and the Whiz Kids. Their vivid recollections also helped me establish the context of race, suburbia, and the counterculture of the 1960s in which the story occurred.

To credit each of them individually would add another chapter to this book. They are all listed among my sources for this story. I am particularly grateful to Michael Thompson, who agreed to meet with me repeatedly so that I could gather his story. I am also grateful to Jerry Barclay, David Wright, Dave Saltenberger, Arnis Rapa, and Dave Esposto for their willingness to dig into their memories of the season.

Finally, I am grateful to my friend Frank Bettendorf and to my wife, Peggy, both of whom encouraged me to believe that the story of Michael and the Whiz Kids was worth telling.

Michael
and the
Whiz Kids

ONE

The Whiz Kids

They sit in one section of the collapsible bleachers that has been pulled out of the gym wall. Nearly twenty of them, all of them tiny, some of them with their dangled feet hardly reaching down to the next row. They are all candidates in 1968 for the "C" basketball team for small players at Crestmoor High in San Bruno, California.

I stand on the gym floor immediately in front of them. I carry a small clump of rolled papers in one hand. When I speak I wield the rolled papers as if they were a blackboard pointer. I wear glasses with heavy frames, white gym shorts, Converse tennis shoes, and a dark-blue jacket with a gold "Coach" stitched on the chest.

"Okay. Listen up," I say. "Fifth period ends at 2:00. We'll practice from 2:00 to 3:30. Only an hour and a half. That means you'll have to run down here to the locker room. There'll be no time to fool around in the I beams playing cootchie with your honey."

They all smile at the idea that one of their teachers knows perfectly well what goes on in the I beams.

"I expect you to change quickly," I say, "and be on the floor in five minutes. You'll have a few minutes to shoot around, get loose. Drills start at 2:15 sharp."

I wait to let them appreciate the precision of my practices.

A bell rings somewhere, signaling the end of sixth period and the school day. Their attention turns to the two small doors of the gym, outside which students hurry to the bus circle. Some of the players squirm, ready to bolt the bleachers.

I tap my paper baton in the air. "You won't hear bells ringing when we practice. But you'll hear my whistle." *With my other hand I pull the whistle from my jacket pocket and hold it up. It is a huge, copper-colored whistle with a mouthpiece so big it hardly fits in my mouth. I clamp it between my teeth and blow it once. Then I remove it from my teeth.* "This whistle is called the Acme Thunderer. Because it sounds more like thunder than a whistle. My father used this whistle in New Guinea during World War II. When he blew it you could hear it in Australia."

They laugh. I put the historic whistle back in my jacket pocket.

"Okay. Some of you played for me last year. Or the year before that. You've gotten very good. That's why you're here."

I smile.

"A few of you can shoot the lights out."

I give no indication of which ones I think that is.

"But the first thing we do at practice is defensive drills. When your attention is at its peak. We go for fifteen minutes, until 2:30."

My defensive drills are infamous. Everybody crouches and shuffles, sliding left and right, back and forth, back and forth, then oblique. I point with one hand at each blast of my Acme Thunderer to indicate changes of direction. After five minutes thighs began to burn. They stumble, fall, struggle back to their feet, and try to keep going. They all know the drills and dread the fifteen minutes of exhaustion.

"Okay," *I say,* "now practice gets interesting."

I pause to let them wonder how.

*"How many of you have ever heard of the Whiz Kids?"
I ask.*

*Not one of them raises his hand. Their faces reflect not
the fascination I had expected, but puzzlement. What do
these so-called Whiz Kids have to do with them? What do
they have to do with basketball?*

*I realize that I have lost them completely. I flash the clump
of rolled papers. "Listen up!" I shout, in an effort to quiet
them and regain their attention. "Some of you sitting there
are hardly five feet tall. I am six two, about half a foot taller
than most of you. I am Gulliver. You are the Lilliputs."*

*They are as puzzled over my reference to Lilliputs as they
were over the talk of Whiz Kids.*

*"You would know who the Lilliputs were," I say, "if I
had had you in my English classes."*

*I have had some of them in my English classes, but they
still don't understand what Jonathan Swift and his book
Gulliver's Travels has to do with them.*

In desperation I return to the subject of the Whiz Kids.

*"Let me explain who the Whiz Kids were. They were five
players from the University of Illinois. They dominated the
Big Ten in basketball for two years in the early forties. They
were the best team in the country. Nobody could beat them.
The Whiz Kids used quickness to hammer better teams. They
could run like deer. They just got the ball and ran. They
scored a lot. Sometimes as many as 90 points a game. They
were way ahead of their time. Watching them fly up and
down the court, a sportswriter said, 'Gee whiz, look at those
kids go.' That's how they got their name. The Whiz Kids."*

*I pause. I have finally gotten their undivided attention. "I
had a chance to see the Whiz Kids play against the University Minnesota when I was just a kid. They were faaaast." I
draw out the word, as if I am describing gunslingers. "You*

are all here because you are small. You get beat up by play-
ground bullies. You can't see the screen in movie theaters.
Even right now, some of you are so short your feet don't
touch the ground."

Several of them kick their legs and laugh.

I continue. "From 2:30 to 3:00 we scrimmage. Full court.
Up and down. Without stopping. The only difference between
you and the Whiz Kids is that you're smaller than they were.
But you're going to go faster than they did." I nod. "They've
got the twenty-four-second clock now in pro basketball. Twenty-
four seconds to get a shot? That's way too long for me. We'll
put up a shot in ten seconds or less. Ten seconds or less!" I put
my Acme Thunderer back in my teeth. "You'll run faster and
shoot faster than anybody in the history of basketball."

They stare at me in disbelief.

I stare back at them. "Okay. Okay. You are the Crest-
moor Falcons. Right?"

They neither nod nor speak.

"What makes a falcon unique?"

None of them knows.

I raise my voice. "A falcon is the fastest creature on the
face of the earth."

So?

"That's what you'll be. The fastest basketball team on the
face of the earth."

It was hard for any of them to believe my claim that as basketball players they would be distinguished in any way. Crestmoor High School? The school was too new to be bragging
that it was an athletic powerhouse.

Nearly every garage in the San Bruno neighborhood had
a backboard nailed to it, but the sloped driveways were
difficult to negotiate. The only place to experience a real
hardwood gym floor was in a recreation center that town

citizens had built. The city's gym rats flocked there on windy nights and rainy weekends for pickup games. But then the Parks Department began charging fifty cents to get into the gym and only those brave enough to figure out how to sneak in found a warm, dry place to play.

From Crestmoor's opening in 1962 the school's athletic teams had struggled. Some blamed the small enrollment or the wind and the fog for all the athletic defeats. Then enrollment hit fifteen hundred but the defeats continued. To minimize the impact of the defeats one of the varsity basketball teams performed as a comic jug band before a packed Little Theater audience. It was, the school paper reported with irony, "an unforgettable performance."

Meanwhile, the mounting basketball losses were also unforgettable. I was hired to teach English and coach basketball when the school opened. It was two years before we won a game. The angry parent of one of the players called me and threatened to shoot me. The first basketball victory came against a school named Lick-Wilmerding. In the smoke-filled teachers' lounge, fellow coaches joked that Lick-Wilmerding was a sexual act, not a school.

In postgame jubilation over the victory, I got up on the school's three-meter diving board and celebrated the victory by diving into the water in my suit. At poolside, my tie dripping like a faucet, I told the sportswriter who covered the landmark victory, "I just hope we haven't peaked too soon."

I began arguing for a school boundary change that would lead to a still-larger student body, taller students, fewer defeats, and no death threats. But other coaches complained that it wasn't the enrollment that led to all the defeats. There was a "negative attitude" among the entire student body. Stop whining, an editorial in the school paper insisted. Play ball! There are enough tall students here already!

But one of them was a six six, unathletic maverick who

walked on campus one morning wearing a stovepipe hat and a swallowtail coat. The administration huddled immediately to try to figure out what to do about the odd behavior. Meanwhile, I asked the maverick if he had ever played basketball. The answer was an abrupt, "No! And I expect to be able to say the same thing when I'm seventy."

The other big man was a giant Tongan with a flat nose, huge hands, and a perpetual smile. He came into the gym one day and spoke to me in fractured English. "I play ball you?" he asked.

I looked him up and down. Here, finally, was the big man I had been hoping for. "How tall are you?"

"Two meter, maybe."

I wondered how tall two meters was, in feet and inches. Could this be the first high school seven-footer on the San Francisco Peninsula?

I bounced a ball at him and told him to dribble the length of the floor with his right hand, then return with his left. He smiled and nodded. Then he went down the floor like a backhoe, some long mechanical arm out ahead of him wrenching him along according to the principles of a lever.

When he handed the ball back to me, he said, "Focking ball too soft."

I wondered if that was because he had punctured it.

Before one game, as a show of what a "powerhouse" they were, the towering opponents began dunking during warmups. Despite my protests the slam dunks continued until the basket sagged and the backboard finally cracked. It took thirty minutes to hang a new basket. In the game that followed the score was 40–5 at halftime. Before I could figure out what to say to my confused players during a halftime pep talk, the team's manager piped up, "Did anybody bring anything to read?"

While the basketball losses mounted, Peninsula newspapers

noted that the new school was better known for its outstanding Homemaking Department, which had placed three girls in the California state bake-off contest. If they didn't win at basketball it was because they "couldn't have cake and eat it too." Finally, in one of the few close games a Falcon player had tried to win the game by hurling a Hail Mary buzzer-beater the length of the floor. The ball disappeared somewhere above the lights and never came down.

Then there was the night the Crestmoor Falcons basketball team proudly trotted onto the floor in brand-new blue satin warm-up jackets with "FALCONS" stitched in gold across the back. It wasn't until after the game—another painful loss—that somebody noticed that one of the jackets had misspelled it "FALCOLS."

This was a team with an English teacher who couldn't spell. This was a basketball program that could produce comic jug bands but not a winning team. Now I was predicting a team whose play would be celebrated. All of those sitting in the bleachers listening wanted to believe me. But I had a reputation for rosy predictions. I had once claimed that one of my star varsity players would be in the NBA someday. A Tuesday-night winter recreation league for six-foot-and-under players was as far as the star got.

I had predicted that they would be the fastest basketball team ever. Better and faster than those Whiz Kids. It seemed not just unlikely, it seemed impossible. It wasn't in the bones or I beams of Crestmoor High. Yet there I stood, as cocksure as General Patton, making just that claim.

"Okay," I say, winding down my speech to my presumed champions, "I've got copies here of the exponent chart." I unroll the clump of papers and begin passing out the sheets to several in the front row. "Pass these around. If you don't understand the point system that determines how your age,

your height, and your weight are used to figure your individual exponents, ask me now."

Nobody speaks. They are all studying the exponent chart.

"Official weigh-ins are in two weeks, before our first league game. Between now and then you can't do anything about your age or your height. It's your weight that matters most. Know your target weight. Memorize it. You all need to be below that weight or right on it in two weeks. If you're over by even a pound, you can't play."

I pause a final time.

"Okay. How many think they might be over their target weight?"

One hand goes up. He is conspicuous not just because he is the only black student at Crestmoor High but because he is the most twiggy and raw-boned among the players sitting in the bleachers.

I look at him. "Michael, you're over your weight?"

"Yes."

"By how much?"

"A few pounds."

"Oh, oh!"

After Michael confessed that he might be a "few pounds" overweight I took my Acme Thunderer out of my pocket and looked confused. The player with slinky moves and a deadly shot that would lead the team to the championship—he might not make weight?

Stories of athletes desperately trying to "make weight" were commonplace. Crash diets, starvation, steam baths as hot and dehydrating as Native American sweat lodges, endless exercise, even spitting in school wastebaskets on the day of weigh-ins—they were the practical measures by which athletes hoped to make weight for exponent basketball or wrestling. But I felt they were not healthy.

"Have you been working out?" I asked Michael.

He hung his head, as if he was confessing now to idleness. "A little."

In fact, that summer he had begun dating one of his Crestmoor classmates. The work of trying to arrange secret liaisons with the girl, whose parents would not have approved of their daughter dating a black classmate, had been a distraction from basketball. On one occasion the girl's mother had come home from work unexpectedly and he had to hide in the girl's tiny bedroom closet. It was then that he realized he was claustrophobic. "The walls are closing in on me," he told himself. "I gotta get out of here."

He managed to escape detection but the challenge of more and more secret liaisons only continued to distract him from basketball. His confession to me that an idle summer had made him overweight was discouraging.

The best I could hope for was that the sudden resumption of sweat-dripping, exhausting practices would bring Michael into the right condition and weight. I put my Acme Thunderer back in my mouth and delivered one quick blast. "All right. That's it. I'll see you all at practice tomorrow. And Michael, start losing that weight *right now*."

TWO

Michael

Michael Thompson was born on a dry, cold day in 1951 in the small town of Madill, Oklahoma. He was the son of a black preacher and a tiny twenty-one-year-old woman named Doris Gibbs, who could track her ancestry all the way back to southern slaves in the Civil War. She christened her son Michael, meaning he was like God. But the preacher left town soon after Michael was born and Doris married Jim Thompson, an Army noncommissioned officer.

One day when he was still an infant his uncle tried to throw him a ball and noticed that Michael's eyes didn't move. There were other signs that something wasn't right with his vision, and Doris and Jim Thompson took the new baby to doctors in Oklahoma City.

The diagnosis was quick and painful. "Mr. And Mrs. Thompson," the doctors said, "your boy is blind."

Back in Madill friends who heard the news tried to minimize the tragedy by remarking, "Well, there ain't much to see in Madill anyway."

Jim Thompson was quiet but forceful. His wife, Doris, was hardly five feet tall but strong-minded. The two of them refused to accept the possibility that their infant son would go through life blind. Over the next five years they drove ninety miles to Oklahoma City sixteen times for operations to restore their son's vision. One of the first things Michael would remember seeing was the ice house in Madill where he went with his quiet father to get blocks of ice. When he was eight his parents took him to New York City and to the top of the Empire State Building. Looking down on New York streets his first words were, "Look at all the toy cars."

The view suggested to him that there was a real world with things in miniature. He had no idea how he would one day be a part of that miniature world himself.

The other reality he could now see was that it was a black-and-white world. In Madill the segregation was stark. Black citizens lived in two separate enclaves on one side of the tracks, whites on the other. It all fit perfectly with the simple, black-and-white world that Michael saw on the screen of the local drive-in theater just outside town.

In their friendly enclave the black men were Slim and Lub, Hilly and Straight Edge and Do Do. After the Civil War pamphlets promised that Oklahoma would be a "black paradise," and the state wound up with more all-black towns than the rest of the country combined. But it was no paradise for the likes of Slim and Lub and Hilly, who worked as shoe-shiners, trash haulers, caretakers, domestics, cotton pickers, wood cutters, and spittoon polishers.

One of those black enclaves was called Oil Mill Hill, so named because it was where the picked cotton was ginned and milled and the seed oil extracted. Meanwhile, Madill itself was not much more than a Main Street, a hotel, a county courthouse, a drugstore, and a post office. It was a humble town, out of the way of civilization. Old-timers could remember only two incidents of historic significance in Madill. In 1930 a farmer disappeared and the family hired a "Negro mystic" to find the body. The mystic promptly led the family to a ditch just outside town where the farmer lay, shot in the head. It was such a miraculous discovery that it hardly seemed to fit what the locals considered the unremarkable qualities of black men. Subsequent news reports of the discovery claimed the miracle had been the work of a "Hindu mystic."

In 1932 an Oklahoma state agent and drunkard named Crocket Long got in a drugstore shootout with a former federal prohibition agent named Wylie Lynn. Crocket entered the drugstore wearing a long, black coat and fired repeatedly at Wylie, who was seated at a nearby table. Wylie leaped from his chair and began fanning his six-shooter. In the brief exchange of gunfire both men were killed.

The hocus-pocus of mystics and the murderous escapades of gunslingers were out of character for a quiet little town like Madill, whose residents feared God and sang his praises from both sides of the tracks. The black Pentecostal church up on Oil Mill Hill was the loudest. Their gospel songs were so spirited that white children in Madill for whom religion was a duty sneaked across the tracks and stood in the early Sunday morning shadows outside the church, listening to the singing and shouting and admiring the conviction.

When Jim Thompson got assigned to an Army base in New Jersey, he and Doris left their son in the care of his grandmother, a churchly woman who worshipped daily and sat on her bed at night praying. She forbade smoking and drinking in the house. She was so respected in Madill for her reverence that everybody, white and black, called her "Auntie," as if they were connected by blood to her goodness.

It was Auntie who raised Michael in Madill. She took him to Sunday school, lectured him on the evils of smoking and drinking, and taught him the virtues of the same daily hard work she did as a domestic for white families in Madill. There was never any talk by Auntie of his early blindness. It was God's will. Meanwhile, all the surgeries to restore his sight had left him with a lazy left eye. It meant that he walked about Madill and went to school with his head down and cocked slightly, so that his good right eye became his guide.

When he was nine Auntie took him cotton picking for the first time. All the black pickers gathered in a one-room shack at the edge of a flat field. At the end of the day his fingers were bloody and he was soaked with sweat. He had a full sack of cotton, for which he was paid a quarter. It was, he thought, a meager reward, and the next day he refused to go picking. Auntie spanked him and scolded him for not appreciating the virtues of hard work, but he held fast to his conviction that hard work with meager rewards was meaningless.

When Michael was in the fourth grade in Madill, Jim Thompson retired from the Army and he and Doris headed for California in search of new opportunities for themselves and their son. They left Michael in Madill in the temporary care of Auntie, with assurances that as soon as they found work and an apartment in San Francisco they would send for him.

It was nearly a year before Auntie packed him a bag of sandwiches, took him to the Madill train depot, and then sobbed as she hugged him and waved goodbye to him through the train window. He sat at the same window seat all by himself the entire three-day trip, munching the sandwiches Auntie had packed for him. The sight of him traveling all by himself when he hardly looked big enough to be in school brought occasional passengers to his seat to try to make conversation with him. But he had developed the habit of silence and he spent most of the three-day trip sitting up in his seat and staring out the window, as if the familiar landscape and people of Madill would disappear forever from his life if he left the window from which he had last viewed them.

His mother and father hugged him when he arrived at the train depot in Oakland. Those hugs reflected their hope that life for him in California would be more promising than in the black-and-white, segregated world of Madill. But their first apartments in the black Fillmore District of San Francisco brought much of the same aggravation and bitterness that had caused them to leave Madill.

All of Michael's new friends were black. They walked the Fillmore District streets in packs. Jim and Doris Thompson watched what was happening to their young son and feared that the isolation of the Fillmore would draw him into a crippling separatism in which the only world where he was comfortable was a black one.

Jim Thompson began looking for a San Francisco suburb where they could buy a home. Meanwhile, Michael discovered the game of basketball. He and his friends played a pickup game called "hunch," first on an outdoor blacktop court in the neighborhood, then at a small gym at the Salvation Army Boys Club, where they charged twenty-five cents for admission and he and his friends played day and night. He was the smallest among them. From necessity and that same quiet but headstrong spirit that had led him to refuse to pick cotton he learned to jump in the air to shoot. When he didn't have a quarter to get into the Boys Club gym, he practiced the shot on the outdoor blacktop court, sometimes late into the evening as a cold fog began to settle over the City.

In the first basketball game he ever played, his team won 22–1. He was the smallest player on the team. But he was quick and tireless. He led his team in scoring and began to believe that he could shoot, despite the limitations of his one bad eye.

One day at Everett Junior High in San Francisco his coach took him aside. "You can shoot," he said. "You can *really* shoot." He might have thought it was awkward praise meant to give confidence to a midget with only one good eye. But Michael took it also as a genuine compliment and began to harbor the conviction that he *was* good. He felt that over time and with much practice he could get really good.

Jim Thompson took a job as a deputy sheriff at the San Francisco County Jail in the hills just west of San Bruno on the Peninsula. After searching for months, in 1962 he found a home he and Doris could afford on Catalpa Street in a subdivision called Rollingwood in San Bruno, approximately fifteen miles south of San Francisco.

It was from only a few miles away that the Portola Expedition had first sighted the slate-flat beauty of San Francisco Bay in 1769. By the 1800s San Bruno had become one of a string of small towns that stretched down the Peninsula like the disconnected figures on a charm bracelet. In the 1860s the railroad had come. Then in 1866 a 119-round boxing match with heavy betting gave San Bruno an identity as a hotbed of gambling. That reputation would one day make the town the site of Tanforan Racetrack and one of the few California cities to license card parlors. A folk tale that claimed San Bruno's creeks flowed with whiskey contributed to the town's rough reputation. Still, San Bruno remained so rural that cows roamed the hills and a third of the population kept billy goats. Then the federal government's selection of sixteen acres of San Bruno land as the site of Golden Gate National Cemetery suggested that the town might turn out to be like neighboring Colma, a city housing the dead instead of the living.

The World War II boom in nearby manufacturing plants brought workers who tried to keep the town's rustic setting by settling in new homes on streets like Maple, Cedar, Chestnut, and Cypress. "Hard Hat" Willie, one of the town's councilmen, lived in a tent house with no running water. His political mantra was that he was the champion of the "little, unheard person."

San Bruno was becoming a working-class town with donut

shops, a theater, and a Main Street. Joe's Pool Parlor was where working men met to play poker and "wash down" their burgers with Golden Glow beer. Families clipped newspaper coupons and box tops. Their kids played in the rolling hills with their BB guns. On hot days they skinny-dipped in the city's reservoir. They had leaf fights and played street football games where a lamppost or a blue car marked the end zone. Adult volunteers put up a huge Quonset-hut-like structure that served as a recreation center. The only restrictions for those kids were "be home by dark" and "don't leave tools out at night."

In the 1950s a second building boom hit San Bruno, which builders advertised as an idyllic community, "a place to begin." A dream home with a two-car garage in a traffic-free neighborhood could be purchased for only $22,500. These were homes for the "junior executive," "the man who has made his mark." It was a city of safe neighborhoods, free of traffic and smoke. There were yo-yo contests for the kids. Families vacationed on the Russian River and enjoyed hayrides and bonfires. San Bruno was close to San Francisco but mostly outside the City's fog belt. It was a place where blue- and white-collar workers could coexist, where men who strung phone lines lived next door to those "junior executives."

Subdivisions sprang up in those once rolling, billy goat hills. The population hit nearly forty thousand. Families came to San Bruno looking for sunshine and a yard. In other towns up and down the Peninsula the same building booms were taking place. It meant that the flat, silver- and-green beauty of the Peninsula that Portola had once stumbled upon was now a jumble of perilous, gridlocked freeways, high-rise hotels, and one community after another—from South San Francisco to Redwood City—crashing together and threatening to squeeze the life and uniqueness out of each other. For those San Bruno kids looking for something exciting there was nothing going south. Adventure lay in San Francisco—in Chinatown, jazz in North Beach, wild music in the Haight-Ashbury.

San Bruno was now neither a city nor rolling countryside. It was a suburb. Perhaps as a legacy of an earlier era of hard hats and little people, it prided itself on being open, accepting, democratic. There was plenty of economic diversity. Doctors, ministers, mail carriers, professors, welders, salesmen, truck drivers—they all lived on the same block. But there was only a sprinkle of minorities, and no blacks. The racism was subtle but painful. Home buyers in some parts of the Peninsula had to sign covenants against selling to non-Caucasians. Just north of Rollingwood, real estate agents for developers showed black families a fake plat map that indicated all the lots were sold. "That way," the agents explained to white buyers, "the feelings of black people aren't hurt."

There were a few racist jokes. Elsewhere, issues of race weren't discussed. The kids went into the City to hear Ray Charles. They listened to soul music on the radio. They saw black kids at dances sponsored by other schools. If there were race problems, they were in the movies or long ago and far away. If parents had racist convictions they kept quiet at the dinner table.

The Thompsons were the first black family in San Bruno. Along with a few Samoan, Tongan, and Mexican families, they were the only minorities in the suburb. The Samoans and Tongans were quickly stereotyped: they were muscular giants and all they wanted to do was roast pigs in pits dug in their backyard. They were tough, brutal fighters. When a white teenager had his expensive Puma basketball shoes stolen, his friends told him, "The good news is we know who stole your Pumas." The bad news, they said, was that the thief was a Samoan. A stand-up, bare-knuckle fight between a Samoan and a muscled white football player in a San Bruno parking lot drew a huge crowd.

Otherwise, San Bruno remained a peaceful, quiet community where families worked hard, spent little, and saved money in order to send their children to college. Some of them had fled the mayhem and violence of the City, and they had come to San Bruno looking for open space instead of houses with common walls. Now they had their safe place and it was fenced in. What few blacks San Bruno kids saw were at athletic contests against City schools.

Outside the quiet bell jar of San Bruno, the Civil Rights era was unfolding. There were nightly TV pictures of cops with truncheons beating black men. There were Civil Rights marches. Black leaders were on the news nightly, calling for nonviolence and an end to discrimination.

The Thompson house in Rollingwood was on the brow of a steep hill and looked down on the white tombstones in neat rows in Golden Gate National Cemetery. The panoramic view of so many graves seemed more of a constant reminder of death than the proper setting for the new life that Jim and Doris Thompson wanted for their son. Their initial reception was as ominous as those tombstones. They had a cross burned on their front lawn one night shortly after they moved in. Their home was egged. Few of the neighbors spoke to them. "There goes the neighborhood," some said.

Doris Thompson grew protective of her tiny son and began ruling over his behavior with an iron hand. Whenever he misbehaved she deepened the tone of her voice and called him "Michael Ralph." Then she would send him to a nearby park to get a willow switch.

One day he came back with a small branch. "What am I supposed to do with that little stick?" she said. "Now go get me a real one." The eventual spanking with a willow switch stung all the way to his feet.

She instructed him that if he experienced racism in the new community he was to ignore it. But she told him repeatedly, "If they hit you, you hit 'em back."

He remained quiet and guarded, especially around his basketball teammates at Willard B. Engvall Junior High, some of whom were already nearly a half foot taller than he was. He felt they had expectations for him of antic, showboat behavior only because he was black. So he played cautiously, without the leaping quickness that he had learned on San Francisco blacktop courts, and he came off the bench only as a sub.

One day a student in one of his classes said, "So you're the only back kid in school."

Yes, he nodded, he was.

"But you're not tall."

"No."

"You don't seem to jump that well."

"No."

"And you don't *look* that fast."

He knew that was true too only because he had played with deliberate caution.

"So what are you doing on a basketball court then?"

"I like to play," he said.

It was in that play that he acquired the nickname Slinky, because he could slip and slide through the smallest opening between defensive players, get himself to the basket, and shoot an easy layup.

How did he do it? they wondered.

He said he didn't know. He just did it.

THREE

Coach

Michael entered Crestmoor High School in San Bruno as a freshman in the fall of 1965. Opened just three years earlier in September 1962, the school was the newest of seven schools in the San Mateo Union High School District. It was situated on forty acres on the crest of a high hill in San Bruno. Tractors scraped a flat top on the hill to make room for buildings and playing fields. The location made it as impenetrable and inaccessible as a medieval castle. The surrounding streets curled and twisted, leading to dead ends and cul-de-sacs.

The new school had been described as having the clean, modern lines of "steel and glass." Its architectural style was called Brutalism because of the school's blocky appearance and I beams on the outside of the walls. It gave the modular structure of the school the cold architecture of an Erector set. Between classes young couples often tried to find some warmth and privacy tucked in one of those many I beams.

The school chose for its mascot high-flying, swift Falcons. For visitors to the school, finding their way up to the Falcons' lair was like negotiating an English hedge maze. A bus driver bringing an opposing team up to the campus once phoned the school. "I can see you up on the hill," he complained. "But how the hell do I get there?"

Despite the inaccessibility of its campus, schools from all

over the Peninsula sent their congratulations to Crestmoor High upon its opening with twenty-six teachers but only five hundred freshman and sophomore students, which was a quarter of the enrollment of the athletic powerhouse schools on the Peninsula.

The month that Crestmoor High opened, astronaut Walter Schirra orbited the earth in an amazing display of American technological power. Midway through the 1962 National League Baseball season, the San Francisco Giants trailed the Dodgers by five and a half games and seemed doomed to defeat, but then they started a miraculous comeback and won the pennant. The opening of the brand-new, $4 million Crestmoor High School after just two years of construction was just as amazing and miraculous.

At first, everybody in the community was excited. The angled corridors, the white-tile floors, and the I-beam construction gave the school an orderly, efficient look. There were bright lights. English teachers had their students read Ernest Hemingway's short story "A Clean, Well-Lighted Place." Students wondered if Hemingway could have been talking about Crestmoor High School instead of a cafe in Paris.

It was a school whose students were described as the "best-dressed on the Peninsula." They were as neat and clean as the school's architecture. And it wasn't just the "little sister" school of crosstown rival Capuchino High, one of those athletic powerhouse high schools on the San Francisco Peninsula. Crestmoor High was a powerhouse in the making. The modern language lab had glass study carrels with earphones for listening to language lessons. The science labs and the art wing had panoramic views of the entire bay. The modular walls meant that classrooms could mutate like huge cells. The little theater had upholstered cushion seats and a sound and light control room for the stage crew.

There were two swimming pools in the center of the school, giving the campus the look of a country club. Early on students gathered on the balcony above the diving pool to throw coins into the water and make wishes. The pool was too deep to see the coins that soon began collecting on the bottom. Then one night at 2:00 a.m., a quiet student who was a scuba diver put on all his diving gear and sneaked into the school by climbing one of the I beams. Once at the bottom of the pool he soon had a fistful of money. But his mother had quickly sensed his absence. When he returned home the San Bruno police were waiting.

It was a comic incident that seemed to give the school character and a resourceful spirit. But by the second and third year negatives were emerging. The steel walls got so hot on sunny days that teachers joked you didn't just cook eggs on the walls, you burned them to a crisp. The girls' bathroom was so smoke-filled it was like "walking into the lobby of a casino." The faculty lounge was worse, a tin cave with no windows and a thick pall of smoke raised by coaches who smoked huge cigars.

When Beatlemania hit, Crestmoor faculty assigned to chaperone the school dances complained of "too much pelvic action" and an "obscene series of gyrations." Then the administration and faculty cracked down on long hair. Students responded by switching distributor wires on cars in the faculty parking lot. Students cracked jokes during serious classroom discussion and threw spitballs. Those students warned to stay out of the I beams because what they did there was vulgar argued that hand holding was not vulgar. And it didn't lead to sex. The I beams were at least someplace to hide from the cold wind.

Even the school hymn was flawed. Celebrating the "gold and blue, gold and blue" of the high-flying Crestmoor Falcons, it was written in the wrong key, and the pep band couldn't play it at games. When they finally did get the pep song in the right key, the wind and fog off Sweeney Ridge to the west howled and blew with such fierceness that students changed the song to "cold and blue, cold and blue."

The faculty were young and outspoken. Some of them saw themselves as theatrical Broadway performers who did five exhausting, fifty-minute acts every day for nine months a year. At the same time, they complained about too many preps, overloaded classes, not enough books, and dull faculty meetings. Coaches protested to the school board that their pay amounted to pennies per day. Led by rebel teachers at Crestmoor High, a small group of district faculty organized themselves into an American Federation of Teachers local and demanded change.

Crestmoor High became the "rough-and-tumble" school. They were the "barbarians" from up on the windy hill. The winds off Sweeney Ridge blew in from left field on the baseball diamond at "hurricane velocity." To stay warm, visiting teams huddled in their bus between innings. Players could throw their warm-up jackets against the cyclone fence and watch them stay pasted there.

Who would live on such a windswept ridge? Who would go to school on such an isolated, remote hilltop? Feeling the isolation, a language teacher drove to the Golden Gate Bridge and dropped a message in a bottle, as if to say, "Is anybody else out there?" It was no comfort to the Hilltoppers when a message came back months later from a remote coral lagoon in Micronesia.

In the fall of 1965, when he entered Crestmoor High as a freshman, Michael Thompson was the only black student in school. He learned to carry a perpetual faint smile that reflected goodwill and a deep warmth. "You learn a whole lot more listening," he would explain himself later, "than you do running your mouth."

That first year at Crestmoor he was just over five feet tall and weighed only one hundred pounds. He sought to enter the mainstream of student activities by signing up to play football. His mother and then the doctors who gave him a physical forbade it. An injury to his eyes could blind him again. It served to remind him for the first time since Madill that he had entered the world blind.

Still eager to be a part of the athletic program, he walked into the Falcons' gym when the lightweight basketball season was already in progress and met me for the first time. I had been born in 1934 at halftime of a basketball game at a small college in Minnesota where my father coached until the war. The halftime birth link was purely coincidental, but it still put basketball in my blood. For as long as I could remember, sometimes for hours on end, I practiced all by myself with my Converse gym shoes delivering rubbery yips like puppies as I chased my own missed shots. I had played and sweated from the gym at that small college in Minnesota, to auditoriums that stank of three-ring circuses and tiger cages, to cavernous Williams Arena at the University of Minnesota, so big they called it "The Barn," to arenas at the foot of volcanoes in Hawaii, to stadiums in California with pep bands, to old abandoned churches in Germany where the pews had been removed and one basket hung in front of an altar where a plaster-of-paris figure of Jesus watched through the glass backboards.

But nothing could have been more novel to me than the sight of a tiny black student wandering into the gym. There had been no black people within miles of the neighborhood in which I had been raised in southwest Minneapolis. My first conversation ever with a black man occurred one fall in 1946, when I was twelve years old, after my father had come home from the war and began working as a counselor at the VA hospital in Minneapolis. His patients were all shell-shocked World War II soldiers. One of them was a black man named Carl Fraction, whom my father invited to join a dozen uncles on a pheasant-hunting trip in southern Minnesota. One of Carl Fraction's legs was still wrapped in white gauze from a shrapnel wound he had received. During the long drive I sat in the backseat with Fraction and had time during the awkward silences to become worried at the prospect of some of my uncles refusing to hunt with a black man. When we finally arrived at the farm those uncles stood in an ominous semicircle with their shotguns broken open and loaded. But the tension disappeared when Fraction, who limped through the cornfields but was a crack shot, brought down the first pheasant on the wing.

When Michael walked into the gym I spotted him immediately. "I'd like to play basketball," he told me.

I looked at Michael, who was small enough to play lightweight basketball. But could he shoot?

I bounced a ball to him. "Let me see you shoot."

Michael wore desert boots and a heavy gray jacket with a fleece collar. He took off his jacket and carefully folded it on the floor. Then he took off his shoes and walked to the free-throw circle in just his socks, turned around quickly, and leaped. He hung in the air a second, holding the ball off his right shoulder, his head cocked.

The net seemed to hiss when the high, arching shot dropped into the basket.

I nodded and smiled. But the mechanics of his shot seemed strange, as if his right arm were a gun barrel he had to aim down by cocking his head.

I walked out to him and handed him the ball. "Again."

The net hissed with the same results.

I now stood face to face with Michael, who had cocked his head to look at me with his good eye.

"I see you've got a bad eye," I said.

Michael shrugged. "It doesn't bother me."

I laughed. "I can see that."

Michael was eager to play basketball, a game he could enjoy without risking blindness. "Is it too late to play?" he wondered.

No, it wasn't too late, I said. "How soon can you get rid of those damn boots?"

The boots and jacket with the fleece collar and secondhand clothes became as much of a uniform for Michael Thompson at Crestmoor High as his basketball jersey and pants. For the next four years he would wear the same outfit nearly every day to school. In time, after he was no longer the cautious gnome he had been at first in San Bruno, he added a narrow-brimmed corduroy fedora to his uniform. He curled the front brim down to give himself a stylish look.

The school accepted him. The community accepted him. But he remained the only black student at Crestmoor, except for a few months each year when his parents took in black girls from San Francisco as foster children. The girls had neither basketball nor Michael's quiet smile to make their way into the society of an all-white school, and they were quickly bitter. One of them was labeled unattractive and had to endure racist insults from boys. White girls came to her defense, but she soon disappeared from the campus. Another girl with light skin and a model's stature had to listen to a boy shout at her as she crossed the Great Court, "You're not bad looking for a nigger." A white student eventually dated her, but he faced hostility from a few of his classmates. "We're just friends," he had to explain. "I'm not gonna marry her."

Then one of Michael's foster sisters received a racial insult so foul that she smacked the girl who had delivered it. It was behavior that seemed consistent with Doris Thompson's warnings to her son. But the parents of the girl who had been hit came to the Thompson house and demanded apologies.

As soon as the girls could find permanent homes in the City, they left San Bruno. It meant that Michael was not only the first black student at the school, he was the only one who came back each year. His circle of friends grew wider and wider. His mother always had dinner ready for him and any of the friends he brought home after school. His favorites were her chili, a delicious gumbo, and a fried chicken that took her two days to prepare.

On those Friday nights around the dinner table, while he inhaled the chicken, his mother delivered admonitions to him about behaving himself at his new school. He was to ignore racial insults, she kept reminding him. Unless somebody hit him, he was never to hit back. It would have been an overworked warning if she hadn't invested each repetition of it with more and more urgency. She wanted him to be prepared for trouble. He protested that he had made good friends at Crestmoor. Nothing had happened! She countered with the argument that it was *because* nothing had happened yet that it would.

Despite his mother's warnings, nothing happened. Around Crestmoor he kept his miniature smile, as if it pleased him as much as his mother that he knew exactly what to do to stay out of trouble. He was quiet and attentive in class. Because he dropped his head to focus with his good eye on whoever was speaking to him, it magnified the appearance of timidity. Still, he made more and more white friends. When those friends got in trouble and were grounded, they begged him to "come over and get me outta the house." The mothers conceded, "You can go anywhere with Michael Thompson." Because he was the responsible one, the mature one. When he had supper with his friends his manners were impeccable. When one of those friends ran away from home Doris Thompson called the runaway's mother to tell her, "Don't worry about your son. I've got him here with Michael."

Those same friends who got into trouble now and then liked to go into the Haight-Ashbury and smoke weed. But he had no interest. "What do I need to go to the Haight for?" he told his friends. "I've seen all that stuff." Besides, his mother trusted him. He could come and go on his own. "She knows who I am," he told his friends, "and what I'm about. She calls the principal of the school once a week to see how I'm doing. If she found out I went to the Haight and smoked dope, she'd kill me."

He laughed at his friends' jokes. One day in the gym, the team manager began performing a jump shot that was a deliberate caricature of an athletic buffoon. Michael fell to the gym floor, laughing so hard that he gagged and they had to pound him on his back.

"My God, he's turning white!" they joked.

He was, but in ways that none of them would have understood. He had come from Madill, Oklahoma, where he had lived in a black ghetto and picked cotton just once before he saw that a segregated life of menial work was no life at all. What his parents wanted for him was what he wanted for himself. It meant listening and looking comfortable even if he wasn't. It meant behaving himself and most of all avoiding the free-spirited, carefree behavior of an Uncle Tom.

It was the game of basketball that was his special passkey to the white world of Crestmoor High and San Bruno. As a tiny freshman, after demonstrating his odd jump shot to me, he became a starter on the "D" team, the smallest of the small, freshmen and sophomores mainly with baby faces and game jerseys that hung on them like sacks. The team didn't win a game. He was just skin and bone but he was still one of the leading scorers because he could slink through the tightest gaggle of sweat-soaked bodies and get himself to the basket.

"How come you always seem to have the ball?" a teammate said.

"The ball comes to the shooter," he answered, not with the pop-off arrogance of a splendid shooter but with the flat voice of a scientist describing a fixed law of nature.

He was only a freshman when he began to entertain the belief that in the years ahead he could work his way up to varsity competition, with the glory of packed gyms and uniforms that fit. He was hardly bigger than a thumb, but he already had a slinky quickness and a deadly jump shot. If he could just grow a little he would be able to hold his own or maybe even get the better of players a foot taller than he was.

The first step in that direction was as a sophomore on the "C" team. His odd jump shot with his head cocked became nearly unstoppable among the other midget players, and he led the team in scoring. But at the end of the season he was only a little taller than he had been as a freshman, and he resigned himself to playing "C" basketball again his junior year. By the time he was a senior, he felt, a late growth spurt and an even deadlier jump shot would help him finally realize his varsity basketball ambitions.

That junior year as a "C" player he scored 30 points in one game. With only seven-minute quarters, it was an astonishing feat. When defenders played him tight to stop his jump shot he used his quickness to slither through knots of players to get to the basket. If he could get just a few inches of clearance from his defender driving along the baseline, he loved to stop on a dime, leap, and draw his rifle bead on just the rim and net, without the larger target of a backboard. He led the league in scoring again and was selected first team All-League. He was, coaches around the league said, "that good black kid from Crestmoor."

But the Falcons didn't win the "C" championship, and after one loss the school newspaper described him as a "dejected figure" in the locker room. They said it was his will to win and not just his shooting or his slinky moves that set him apart. Every time he played he gave maximum effort. It was praise he deserved. "But no effort," he said, "is good enough unless you win."

In April 1968 Martin Luther King Jr. was shot. At lunch the next day student journalists held a "Human Happening" in a classroom packed with students. The organizers wanted Michael to be part of a panel presentation on race. But Michael refused. He didn't like speaking in public, he said. A young black student brought in from the City to express a black perspective predicted that in five years white America would be dead.

It precipitated angry disagreements among the white students, two-thirds of whom said they wanted black teachers and a course in minority history. But one white student insisted in the school paper that all black people who revolt and riot should be killed. Another student disagreed: don't kill them, he argued. Just "shoot to scare them."

The 1968–69 school year began with workshops for all district teachers on black history, assimilation, and institutional racism. At the same time several of the district schools, including Crestmoor, initiated courses for students in minority history. Proof of the need for the courses was reflected in an incident later that spring on the baseball field. In a game against an all-black baseball team from Oakland, one of their players received a nasty spike wound sliding into second base. The Crestmoor coach tried to stanch the bleeding with dark-brown antiseptic gauze. When girls in the bleachers saw the incident, one of them said, "I didn't know they had black blood."

Crestmoor High saw the need for racial understanding. A conference at Crestmoor for all district students took up the subject of de facto segregation in San Bruno. Student leaders for the conference created a fictional Finnish academician named Borgis Ralphus and credited him with strong arguments for integration. Students wrote in the school's newspaper that federal action was required to stop the violence against black demonstrators in the South. Student journalists insisted that blacks weren't to blame for the Watts riots. Blaming them was like "pushing the problem under the rug." Still, some students feared that race riots at nearby Hunter's Point in the City would spill over to San Bruno.

For Michael the game of basketball was a bell jar within a bell jar. The hatred that had prompted the assassination of Martin Luther King reflected animosities that had no place on a basketball team. Basketball was a democracy. All players were not created equal, either in talent or in character. But what differences there were had to be ignored.

The summer before his senior year Michael put on a few pounds so that his ribcage no longer wrinkled his chest like a washboard. In the early part of the summer, to get his legs in shape for the upcoming basketball season, he jogged the steep hills up to his home in Rollingwood. At first he could make it only halfway up Catalpa before he had to stop and rest. But by the end of the summer he could go to the top at a near-sprint. His legs, he told himself, had never been in better shape.

He spent many days that summer working on his slinky moves and stopping quickly for his jump shot. He felt that his quickness, his jump shot, and his strong legs would be his ticket to varsity play. But the growth spurt he was hoping for never came. And as the opening of school approached, those small players who had already decided to play "C" basketball tried to persuade him not to wait until winter to play varsity basketball. "The 'C' team's gonna be good," they told him. With Michael they would be "a hell of a team. If we don't get too many injuries, we'll win it."

He insisted that his goal had always been to play varsity his senior year.

"The varsity won't be any good," they said. "They probably won't win a game."

His eagerness to play varsity basketball began to fade. "Well, I don't like to lose."

"We'll be good playing together. We can win it all," they repeated.

"That's my goal," he said, "to win a championship." His height and age were right for him to play "Cs", he said. But despite his hill workouts he had gained a little weight over the late summer. "I don't think I can lose the weight."

They could see he was wavering. "We'll help you lose it. You gotta play 'Cs'. We'll be a hell of a team."

FOUR

Suitcase and the Professor

There are six baskets, two at either end of the Crestmoor gym, with glass backboards like bookends for the full court, then two short sideways courts with four fan-shaped metal backboards. Steel girders run across the ceiling and along one of the walls, giving the gym the faint smell of iron. Otherwise the gym is odorless and colorless. Halogen lights hang from the ceiling like small steeple bells. The lights take ten minutes to come on and illuminate the gym like a prison yard. Only the bright blue of crash mats hanging on the wall behind each main basket break the monotony of the cream-colored walls.

When the gym is empty the only sound is from two huge ceiling heaters that seem to be purring softly like cats. But when the bleachers are packed the noise from screaming fans is deafening. At the far end there is a score clock high up on the wall. Beside the clock is a small red buzzer with a bell horn. When it sounds at the end of a close game it is supposed to cut through the crowd noise and signal that the game is over. But the noise is usually so loud that in the early days of the school a faculty member who had never seen a basketball game was given the extracurricular assignment of sitting at the end of the scorer's table and firing a starter's pistol to end the play. When the pistol failed, the faculty member ran onto the court holding the pistol in the air and shouting, "Stop! Stop! Stop!" as he dodged through the players.

Along the far wall of the gym hang blue pennants for the championships won by Crestmoor teams. After six years of competition involving over a hundred teams there are only two pennants hanging from the wire like animal fangs, one for wrestling and one for swimming.

I stand now at one of the free-throw lines of the main court, my whistle in my mouth, a three-by-five card in one hand. There are players at each of the six baskets, moving and shooting from every angle and distance. I turn slowly, as if I am a figure on a lazy Susan, my eyes stopping for a few seconds on each player to watch him shoot. I check the thick watch on my right wrist, an Actua Chronograph with a sweep second hand that can be started and stopped and that my father carried to war in the South Pacific along with the Acme Thunderer whistle.

At exactly 2:15 I blow my whistle. "Gather up!" I shout.

There are just ten of them now, half the number that sat in the bleachers the day before. They gather around me at the center-jump circle, dripping sweat. I look at the three-by-five card. "Okay. We'll start with the ground rules for the ten-second offense. Here's the main rule you want to keep in mind: when we scrimmage, if your team doesn't put up a shot in ten seconds after you get possession of the ball, I blow my whistle"—I pause to give a blast on the whistle, and some of them laugh and jump back—"then you give up the ball. Just drop it wherever you are. The defense picks up the loose ball and down they go, a shot in ten seconds, or they give it up. This is after baskets, free throws, turnovers—whenever. When you take possession of the ball, you run, run, run. Everybody with me so far?"

They all are and several of them bounce the balls they are holding, as if they are anxious to put into practice what I have just explained.

"Okay. Rule two. As soon as our opponents put up a shot, we release one player. He's gone. He doesn't wait for the rebound. He's off down the floor."

It is a variation of the "sleeper play," nearly as old as sport itself. The hope is that the opponent won't spot the "sleeper" and cover him at the far end of the court. Or, if they do, it will leave only eight players on the rest of the floor, which will open up the full court for the Falcons to pass and run.

"Who's still in?"

They all nod.

"Okay. Who is the most important person to get us all going?" I don't wait for them to answer. "It's not the guy who winds up shooting in ten seconds. It's the guy who throws the first pass after we get the ball. After rebounds, baskets, free throws, turnovers, any time."

I step to take a ball from one of the players surrounding me. I bounce it. "Some of you may be pitchers in baseball and think you've got a good, strong arm. But a basketball," I say, holding it up high and letting it bounce, "weighs four times what a baseball weighs. Whoever makes that first pass for us has to have a rifle arm. He's got to be accurate too. So let's see who we might be talking about."

I move to one end of the floor and stand along the baseline. One by one each of the ten players stands behind the baseline at the other end of the floor and throws a long pass to me. Some of them are rainbow tosses that scrape the ceiling heaters. Others hardly make it to half court. Some are way wide of the target, me. One bounces and then dribbles out the gym door.

I watch the ball roll out the open door. "Good shot!" I shout, and they all laugh.

I wait. All of my commitment to a ten-second offense, which turns on the ability of at least one of the players to make a rifle pass the full length of the court, seems lost. If *they can't make the threat of getting a quick, deep pass to the release man, opponents won't even bother covering him. It will leave the Falcons trying to play defense shorthanded, as if they are a hockey team trying to skate out a penalty.*

Then the final player steps up to throw. He has long, blond hair that hangs in his face in shags that he keeps out of his eyes by flicking his head frequently. He has narrow shoulders and his arms are long but bony. He hardly seems the candidate I am looking for to make that full-court rifle-shot pass.

He moves up against the gym wall behind the baseline and bounces the ball. Then he hops on his back foot twice, takes one long step, and throws, his arm snapping like a bullwhip. The ball travels in a nearly flat trajectory the length of the gym and then smacks into my hands.

I smile. "All right. Again. This time without all that crow hopping. You're wasting time."

Again he throws, this time without the hops. Again the ball flies like a huge leather bullet.

I nod. "Okay," I shout, "we've got who we want."

His Latvian name was Arnis, but around Crestmoor he was Harry. His mother, Skaidrite, was born in Latvia in 1926, the eldest child of a physician in the city of Riga. She was just fourteen in 1940 when Russia swallowed up the Baltic states. In 1941 the Germans invaded Latvia, "liberating" them from Russian occupation. Skaidrite watched anxiously as her father was among the thousands of Latvian citizens and intellectuals who faced deportation by Nazis to Germany to work as forced laborers. In July 1944 Russian troops coming from the east drove the Germans back out of the Baltic states. Again, Skaidrite's father faced deportation or death, this time as a bourgeois intellectual.

Skaidrite and her family gathered what few possessions they could and managed to board the last train out of Russian-occupied Latvia and get to Dresden, Germany, which was in smoking ruins from the Allied firebombing. Meanwhile, the Russians were approaching Dresden from the east, and the family had to flee again, this time to Annaberg, Germany, where Skaidrite's father was put to work sewing up shrapnel wounds and performing amputations on wounded German soldiers.

When it was clear that Russian troops were now about to overrun Annaberg, Skaidrite fled in the middle of the night with her parents, her twin brothers, and her three-year-old sister. They were on foot, pushing a wooden cart with all their belongings and a baby buggy with the three-year-old.

After a month of walking, still pushing the cart and the baby buggy, Skaidrite and her family finally reached historic Rothenberg, one of the few walled cities still standing in Europe and then occupied by American troops. They took refuge in a camp for displaced persons just outside Rothenberg. They were, Skaidrite thought, safe at last.

But one morning the mayor of Rothenberg told them that all displaced persons from Russian territories were being forcibly repatriated to Russia. It meant the threat again of forced labor camps in Siberia, or worse, torture and firing squads.

Skaidrite and her family fled once more and managed to make their way by foot again, this time to the port at Marseille, where they secured passage on a freighter to Venezuela, the only country accepting displaced persons and their families. Once in Venezuela they immediately began applying for visas to get to America.

One day in Caracas Skaidrite happened to be window shopping with her twin brothers when a woman overheard their conversation in Latvian. The woman invited Skaidrite to visit her boardinghouse with a small room and one bed, where immigrant Latvian men took turns sleeping. Twenty-nine-year-old Roland Rapa, who had also escaped from Russians and then Nazis in war-torn Europe, was one of the men she met.

Skaidrite and Roland were married in Caracas, Venezuela, in 1949. Arnis "Harry" Rapa, their second son, was born in 1953. In 1958, when Arnis was six, the family received visas to come to the United States. For two years in New York City Arnis struggled to learn to speak English and take on the habits of American youth.

In 1962 the family packed suitcases and a station wagon and trailer with their belongings and they headed cross-country for California, camping along the way. Once in California Arnis's father got a job working for United Airlines in San Bruno. The family moved into an old Victorian home in lower San Bruno that was soon redolent with the smell of Latvian sauerkraut and sweet-sour rye bread. In school Arnis spoke in halting sentences, as if he was still struggling with English. But he quickly shed the look of an awkward immigrant and took on the latest styles in teenage dress. He learned to play volleyball, basketball, and baseball, even though his Latvian parents had little interest in American sports.

When he entered Crestmoor as a freshman in 1967 he was five feet seven and weighed only 120 pounds. He was the giant among his "D" basketball teammates and he was one of the team's leading scorers.

Coaching him when he was a tiny freshman, I was confident he would grow, maybe to six feet or more. He had speed and Latvian toughness and a relentless desire to gather-in rebounds. He would have all the skills to be a good varsity player. To hurry that along I put him to work that winter as a varsity manager, where he was always the first one to be on the floor shooting and the last one to leave.

In the fall of 1968, as he stood in the gym listening to me

talk about the ten-second offense, he was one of the best shooters on the team. They could have nicknamed him Dead-eye, because his head flick to get that shag of hair out of his eyes was a prelude to every shot. But one of his teammates hung the nickname Suitcase on him. It fit perfectly, because his family had come halfway around the globe, by train, ship, and on foot, pushing wooden carts and baby carriages, from Latvia to Germany to France to Venezuela to New York to San Francisco, finally to San Bruno, with no more belongings than would fit in a suitcase.

Suitcase's bullwhip arm makes it clear that he is just the player to start the fast break with long bullet passes to his teammates. Now the question is who will be the best release man, who will be the best "sleeper" who can catch those bullet passes? Which one of the players gathered around him can avoid being knocked down like a ten pin by Suitcase's passes?

I decide that the best candidate to be the release man would be the smallest player on the team, and the player least likely to be gathering-in rebounds. That is a senior nicknamed the Professor, because he wears heavy frame glasses that make him look scholarly.

He is five feet five inches tall and weighs one hundred pounds. He is such a tiny figure that he would have no presence at all on the floor if it weren't for those heavy glasses and a thick head of coal-black hair that hangs in shags during the action of a game.

His name was David Wright. He was born in Missouri in 1951, the son of a classically trained pianist who played Chopin along with jazz and ragtime in the house. In Joplin, Missouri, he attended an integrated school and took the presence of black classmates for granted. His first crush was on a black third-grade classmate who never seemed to notice him.

In 1961 the family moved to San Francisco and the Professor was rattled by the fact that black classmates considered the tiny new kid with glasses fair game. After numerous fights, his father enrolled him in a boxing program where he learned to use his jabbing quickness to defend himself. Eventually, the family moved to a home on the San Francisco Peninsula. The Professor's father continued to play classical music in the afternoon, then in the evening to sit with jazz musicians who stopped by to jam late into the night.

The Professor did not touch a basketball until late in the eighth grade. He could neither dribble nor shoot and for him the purpose of basketball was to be at the center of the game, chasing after the ball wherever it went, while the backboard and baskets were just boundaries for that game of pursuit in which he was always at the center of the action.

When he discovered baseball he found that the role of pitcher fit perfectly with his idea of being at the center of the action. At first he was so tiny a figure that opponents shouted that he was just a "baseball cap on the mound." But his control and a baffling curve ball soon earned him the respect of older players who acted as bodyguards for the pint-sized pitcher who could throw strikes.

He did not learn the real point of basketball until the winter before he entered Crestmoor High. In the San Bruno Park gym he and his friends had seen Janis Joplin perform. It was also where the San Francisco Warriors practiced. The sight in the gym of such a small but celebrated figure as Janis Joplin or the Warriors' sparkplug guard Al Attles helped him to realize that a basketball court, if he could learn the game, could provide athletic thrills as exciting as a baseball diamond. He practiced for hours, shooting from various spots on the floor, stopping only to use his T-shirt to wipe the fog off his glasses. He practiced dribbling with either hand so that he could change directions in a flash. He sat watching the Warriors' Jeff Mullins stop quickly off a dribble, then leap and shoot. As soon as the Warriors ended their workouts he practiced dribbling at full speed from midcourt, then stopping on a dime and leaping to shoot. He practiced moving farther and farther away from the basket, at first lunging into the shot just to get it there but gradually developing a smooth, effortless bank shot that drew upon the same sense of rhythm and continuous motion that had made him a good pitcher.

The family moved to Rollingwood, where classical and jazz music continued to pour from the house. Michael and his family were only a few blocks away, and one morning the two boys found themselves side by side in the front seat on the morning bus to Crestmoor. They exchanged brief and awkward hellos, then rode in silence until a hulking older student boarded the bus and stood over Michael.

"You should be in the back of the bus," he told Michael.

Michael stared straight ahead and remained silent.

The Professor stood up in his seat. He hardly came to the hulk's chest. "What the hell are you talking about?"

"Niggers ride in the back of the bus," the hulk insisted and then pointed.

The malice behind the insult was only a variation of those antagonisms the Professor had had to defend himself against when he had first arrived in San Francisco. No matter who displayed it, he felt, there was no place for it in his world.

He stepped into the aisle of the bus, prepared to use his jabbing quickness if he had to, this time to defend his new friend. Before he had to the bus driver stopped the bus and threw the hulk off.

FIVE

Jack Armstrong and Salt

They are all gathered around me again at the center of the floor, each of them dribbling a basketball. "All right," I say, "listen up."

The erratic dribbling stops. The only sound in the gym is those ceiling heaters purring.

"We're gonna scrimmage. Full court. Five on five. Blue versus gold."

They are all wearing reversible T-shirts, blue on one side, gold on the other. I indicate the five players I want to be blue and the five I want to be gold. While some of them switch their T-shirts, I continue. "I want you to move. And remember. If you don't get a shot in ten seconds, you'll hear my whistle. That means give it up. Whoever has the ball, stop where you are. Put the ball on the floor. Get back on defense. Okay. Let's go."

They race up and down the floor, missing one shot after another while I stand at the sidelines ready to deliver a deafening blast on my Acme Thunderer to stop the action.

Two minutes into the drill the blue team rebounds a missed shot and flies down the floor. After two long passes one of the blue players drives into the key and leaps. The gold players collapse on him. But he seems to float through them like a windblown blue soap bubble. Then he is free, only a few feet from the basket with an easy shot.

But instead of shooting he whips a pass out to the Professor on the perimeter.

My whistle sounds.

The Professor quickly puts the ball on the floor.

Several gold players rush to pick it up and go.

"Hold it! Hold it!" I walk to the blue player who just floated to the basket like a soap bubble. I lift one arm and turn my wrist so all the players can see the watch. "That was ten seconds with no shot." I look at the blue player. "What were you waiting for?"

The blue player stares at my watch.

"Why did you pass the ball out?"

He passed, he says, because the Professor was wide open.

"But you had a good shot!" I say.

There is no sign of agreement or disagreement.

"You could have passed the ball until next Sunday and you wouldn't have got a better shot than the one you passed up."

This is a criticism directed at all of the blue team, because all of them had passed up shots. But I continue to face the blue player who is still staring at my watch. "Are you a shooter?"

He doesn't hesitate. "Yes."

"Who told you that?"

He grins. "You did, Coach."

"Why did I tell you that?"

He has no answer.

"I told you that because you can really shoot. Your floater is unstoppable."

He smiles.

"That means when you have a shot, you shoot." I repeat it slowly for the benefit of all of them. "When—you—have—a—shot, shoot!"

It is exactly what they all want to hear, and none more than the blue player I have just singled out.

He was the fourth of the Whiz Kids. His name was Jerry Barclay, but I thought of him as a miniature Jack Armstrong, the all-American boy who was good in the classroom, ate Wheaties for breakfast, had alert eyes and an engaging smile, and performed heroic deeds against arch villains.

He was born in 1953 on the Peninsula. His parents were among the first home buyers in one of the new subdivisions in the San Bruno hills. A deep ravine across the street from his house had wild buckeye trees and coyote brush that served as the same jungle setting in which Jack Armstrong enjoyed heroic adventures. When older playmates from his street started school ahead of him, he found himself bored with solitary games and he pestered his mother so regularly about starting school that she enrolled him early in kindergarten. It meant that he was always the youngest and smallest child in his elementary classes. He was also the most eager to learn.

His aging grandmother, who had been born in 1881, lived with them and complained regularly that the world was going to pot. Proof of it was that "Negroes," even if they weren't on their street yet, were everywhere. His grandmother's complaints would have made him suspicious of anybody who did not look like him if it hadn't been for his father, who had come from the Midwest to California in the Dry Thirties. He was a practical man who could fix anything and worked as the service manager for a San Bruno car dealer, where one of his best mechanics was a Japanese American who had been interned during the war.

"All people deserve respect," his father said with anger over what had happened to his Japanese mechanic. "*All* people," he repeated, to make it clear that he wasn't just talking about his mechanic or his all-American son.

His father's lesson took hold and among his first San Bruno friends were a Japanese American kid named Darrell Hirashima, who was even smaller than he was, and a Canadian immigrant who towered over all of them. They rode bikes everywhere and played tackle football with such ferocity that they had to stop playing when they started to hurt each other.

Meanwhile, his father had no interest in sports and thought the pinnacle of competition was a game of tug-o-war with a dozen husky men opposing each other on a long rope stretched so tight it thrummed like a bass fiddle if anybody plucked it. It was no game for a lightweight who hadn't yet cracked a hundred pounds.

It was his brother, seven years older than he was and himself a fine athlete, who helped make him into a fierce competitor by beating him regularly at Monopoly and chess. Then he would take his little brother outside to their garage basket and beat him there.

His first team play at basketball was at Willard B. Engvall Junior High, which suggested a student body of gawkish nerds. For him it was partly true. He was a straight-A student and in basketball he couldn't make a layup and he had to stand still to dribble. He seldom got in games and did nothing to suggest that he had a future in basketball. But using the Los Angeles Lakers' Jerry West as his role model, he learned to jump into the air and then hang there for a second, his legs straight and loose, until he suddenly tripped the spring that seemed to be holding back his cocked arms. By the time he entered Crestmoor as a ninth grader, at just five feet two inches and 120 pounds, even players a foot taller than he was couldn't stop the shot.

He was an All-League "D" player as a freshman. He could score from outside on his jump shot but also from the inside, relying on what he called his "floater," in which he leaped horizontally instead of vertically and then floated through defenders until he found a clear shot. He was still much shorter than most of his teammates, but despite his size he had every reason to believe that as a junior he would step into a starting role on the varsity.

He was leading the frosh-soph team in scoring when he landed after one of his floaters and wrenched his knee. He had to be carried to the bench. That night doctors told him that the cartilage in his knee had snapped like a rubber band. They operated immediately. For weeks he hobbled around Crestmoor with crutches and a cast. With no more basketball in his life he immersed himself in his studies and campaigned to be president of his class his junior year. He was Jack Armstrong, the all-American boy on crutches. The combination of pluck and vulnerability proved appealing and he won the election easily.

By the time he was a junior in the fall of 1968, despite his school leadership responsibilities, it was still basketball that captured his heart. His plan was to play varsity basketball that year. He was young and small, but he looked forward to Friday night games with pep bands, scripted cheers, and a gym so packed with fans that if you dribbled down the sidelines you could smell the beguiling teenage lipsticks.

It was the Professor who convinced him that summer to forego varsity competition and play "C" basketball instead. They were on the outdoor courts at Crestmoor one hot day that summer, dripping sweat, when the Professor told him exactly what he had told Michael: "We'll be a good team."

He knew it was true.

"It'll be fun . . . playing on a good team." It went without the Professor saying it that there had been no good basketball teams at Crestmoor.

He explained that he had been planning and working all summer to play varsity. He had developed confidence in his "floater" shot. He knew he could score with it against any defenders, short or tall.

"The best you'll do on varsity," the Professor said, "is win half your games."

He still wasn't convinced. He had grown a little over the summer. He doubted now that he could make the exponents.

"You're young," the Professor reminded him of what had been the case since kindergarten. "And you're no bigger than I am. You can make the exponents. We can win the championship!"

"Okay," I say. "Listen up."

Half of them are bent over, trying to catch their breath, their chests heaving from the nonstop pace.

"We've got three rules," I say and hold up three fingers. "Rule one. We release a man every time our opponent shoots. If the shot is good," I say and point to Suitcase, "you snag the ball out of the net before it bounces. Then you step out of bounds and look deep for the Professor."

Suitcase nods.

If the Professor isn't open, I explain, then Suitcase is to look for Michael or Jack Armstrong at half court.

Suitcase nods again.

"Rule two. We shoot before ten seconds are up. I expect to see a few forced shots as you try to beat the clock. That's okay. It's the price we'll pay for dictating the pace of the game."

I pause and lift one hand to show the face of my Actua Chronograph. "In games you won't have this watch or my whistle to tell you to give up the ball. But the watch on my wrist will be ticking away. For all of you."

They wait for rule three.

"Rule three. Once we get the ball on a turnover or a rebound or after they score, we head down the floor. I don't care who goes where. This isn't an Arthur Murray dance studio, with footsteps pasted on the floor so you'll know where to move. This is a gym! This is a basketball court, approximately eighty feet by forty. Think of it as a hardwood

universe. There will be plenty of room for you to improvise and scramble."

I pause.

"None of you knew the story of the Whiz Kids. So how many know the story of the tortoise and the hare?"

They all raise their hands.

"I don't want you guys to be tortoises. I want you to be hares. I know what the basketball sages will say. That I'm crazy. Well, probably, a little." They all laugh. "But it's crazy for a purpose. To have some fun."

They are all dripping sweat, some of them still bent over.

I stop to let them catch their breath so that the import of what I have just said can sink in. Then I ask, "Okay. Questions?"

The fifth blue player raises his hand. He is breathing deeper and harder than the rest. But he is also standing straight and smiling. I think I have just delivered an inspirational speech that is about to be acknowledged with a loud "Huzzah!" by the fifth player.

"Coach," the fifth player says, "can we get a drink?"

His name was David Saltenberger, but to avoid the confusion over two Davids on the same team, I thought of him as Salt, because he was the salt of the earth, reliable and utterly without pretension. He was also quiet and smart, both in class and on the court, as if he knew his role on the team was to be the humble, unsung hero.

As a sophomore just turned fourteen, he was the youngest player on the team. But at five feet ten inches he was also, along with Suitcase, the tallest. Beyond the fact that he had athletic brothers and lived on a steep hill in Rollingwood, he seldom talked about his family, not because he wasn't proud to be a Saltenberger but because he was uncomfortable with any assertions that might sound like boasting.

He had first learned to play basketball at a neighbor's garage court where they played with a whiffle ball that they had to pitch at the basket to score. He had the best jump shot on the team, which he developed playing one-on-one at a garage basket with a slight slope so that he had to shoot with a high arch. I thought of it as a "rainbow shot," but it was very quick and deadly accurate. The only problem was getting him to shoot it.

My mandate had been, "When—you—have—a—shot, *shoot!*" If there was one player on the team who might have had difficulty doing just that, it was Salt. It was not in his unassuming, soft-spoken character to be quite that unrestrained as a basketball player. That was the province of Michael, whose basketball talents Salt stood in awe of. It was Michael who could rebound and dribble the length of the floor, weaving and dodging his way through players, then shoot and score.

Yet Michael was as humble and unassuming as Salt was. It flew in the face of what little Salt knew about blacks. His only contact with them had occurred one night in the Fillmore in San Francisco, when he was mugged by three hoodlums a foot taller than he was. "Give us your money!" they had demanded. He gave them everything he had, even turned his pockets out to demonstrate that he had no intention of defying them.

Defiance and assertiveness weren't in his character.

The only time he had ever come close to them was to settle the issue of who had the quickest shot on the team.

"I'm the fastest," the Professor had said.

Salt quietly took issue with him. His rainbow shot may have traveled a circuitous path to the basket, but his release of the shot was lightning quick.

I knew that an occasional lively side contest was always welcome relief from the exhausting wind sprints and repetitious drills of practice. I often pitted myself against the whole team in free-throw shooting, challenging them to make as many in a row as I could. Or I had the players pair up and happily fight it out as two-man teams in a game of "twenty-one," with only long shots and layups.

Now I sought to settle the matter of who had the quickest shot by staging a shoot-out between the Professor and Salt, with the rest of the team watching.

The two of them took turns crouching, then shooting from the free-throw line while I timed them with my Actua Chronograph.

When they were done the team wanted to know who was the fastest.

My insistence that it was a tie was received with a chorus of boos.

As quick as Salt could shoot, and as accurate as he was with his rainbow shot, it was the grind of aggressive rebounding that gave him the most pleasure. For the season ahead only one or two schools would have lightweight players taller than Salt. He and Suitcase would crash the boards on offense or defense, pull in the rebound, then look for the rest of the Whiz Kids to get the ball to.

I liked nicknames. It was a legacy of my own nickname in high school, when my teammates called me Gangles because my legs grew so fast that they said I looked like a beach ball with two long pipe cleaners stuck in it.

Now it was nicknames that I believed captured the uniqueness of each of the players on my "C" team: an immigrant nicknamed Suitcase, a little bespectacled Professor, a dauntless Jack Armstrong, and a humble Salt.

Only one of them needed no nickname to separate him.

He was a half-blind black pathfinder weaving and dodging his way through a white world. He wasn't "Slinky" or even

"Mike." He was "Michael," suggesting a dignity and pride that he sought every day of his young life.

What they all had most in common was their love of the game of basketball and their size. In a basketball world increasingly dominated by giants, they were all tiny Whiz Kids.

SIX

Zinji

It hadn't always been a world of Goliaths. Among the first gnomes was Zinji, whose mother, Lucy, had a face like Andy Gump, the chinless comic strip character. Lucy was only three feet six inches tall but heavily muscled. Her son Zinji inherited the curse of his mother's size--he was just over four feet tall. But he also inherited the blessing of her muscular legs. He could run and leap all day without tiring, and like many good basketball players, he could swivel his neck so that he seemed to have eyes in the back of his head. Still, if someone had handed him a basketball 2.5 million years ago when he lived on the plains of Africa, he wouldn't have known what to do with it.

A hundred thousand years later *Homo habilis*, otherwise known as Handyman because he could work with tools, wasn't much taller than Zinji. It took another million years before the first five-footers, Peking man and the wide-shouldered Neanderthal, came along.

As if there was a leavening agent in life that kept humankind growing and growing, by three thousand years before Christ the average height of men was up to five feet three inches. Four thousand years later, during the Middle Ages, when mighty generals like Gustavus Adolphus came sweeping down on Europe, his warriors averaged an imposing five feet eight inches.

By the late 1600s the poor peasants of Europe decided that they had had quite enough of mighty warlike behemoths and European height shrank back to five feet five inches. The retreat left Cheyenne Indians, at five feet ten inches on average, among the tallest people in the world. But not for long. White men were soon nearly as tall, and in pursuit of their "manifest destiny" they were as eager to conquer and rule as those mighty generals of the Middle Ages had been.

By 1900 Americans were among the world's tallest people. What was it that made them so tall? Their fat turkeys? A cultural infatuation with stature that led to selective breeding? A continental abundance that led to prosperity and growth? Or were they just a global anomaly, as random as the pygmies of Borneo or the giant Watusi of Burundi?

Whatever the reason, when Dr. James Naismith introduced basketball to Americans in 1892 it was soon obvious that the game favored Leviathans. The early versions of basketball also favored brutes, and the first game in California featured two teams of twenty-five players each. In the subsequent melee, one player committed 118 fouls.

Forty years later it wasn't advantage enough just to be a fierce competitor. It was towering players who made a difference in the game. One of the first was George Mikan, who played for the old Minneapolis Lakers and had to fold and bend himself up like a paper clip just to get in a car. Then came a six-foot-nine-inch, hollow-cheeked stork with the improbable name of Bevo, who played in a gym called "the hog pen" at a small college in Ohio and who scored 116 points in a single game.

In California they had seen the disappearance of the little man in basketball coming, and as far back as the 1920s they had made provisions for leagues and competition that excluded the big man. In December 1922 a basketball prophet named Dr. H. R. Stoltz proposed a system of classification for young athletes, with numerical "exponents" or points figured on the basis of height, age, weight, and semester in high school.

To ensure fairness in the administration of the system, the height was to be taken without shoes, the weight to be figured without clothes, and the exponents for each player were to be determined in the first two weeks of each semester. Dr. Stoltz next proposed four classes of competition—"D," "C," "B," and "A"—based on those numerical exponents. After the exponent calculations were made for each athlete, he could compete at any exponent level higher than his classification, but not lower. A tiny "D" player could play anywhere *up* the alphabet scale, but a tall "A" player could not drop down to compete against shorter players. The effect in basketball was to level the playing field. Or more precisely, to create leagues without giants.

By the 1930s the California Interscholastic Federation further refined the system. They dropped the category of exponents based on semester in school, and fractions in height and weight were to be disregarded. Despite the refinements, it was a system of basketball for the little man that would take hold only in selected parts of the country, where high school districts were flush enough to afford the expenses of additional teams.

There were soon little men in basketball who became as legendary and heroic as their towering counterparts. Asian players who once were thought to be too stunted for basketball now had a game that accommodated their speed and quickness. Their appearance at basketball tryouts confused some coaches.

"Chan," one of those coaches said, "what are *you* here for? To do the team laundry?"

"Coach," Chan answered, "my father's a physicist."

The new peewees in the game acquired nicknames like

Cricket and Mouse, eventually Tiny and Spud and Mugsy. In San Francisco, five feet five inch Willie Wong prompted chants of "Woo Woo" from the fans every time he scored. A championship lightweight team in San Francisco was dubbed "The Big Brown Machine," an irony meant to suggest that a team of little players could be a juggernaut. In the NCAA tourney of 1944 a small Japanese American player named Wat Mikasa, a "whiz kid with the jive drive," led the Utah Utes to the NCAA Championship. He was, New York newspapers reported, the "darling" of the fans. It seemed to be affection meant for somebody whose days were numbered.

Beyond the immediate glory of competition on a level playing field the teams also served as a training ground for players who would one day grow, perhaps not into the lofty figures that the game increasingly seemed to favor, but into speedy players who could at least hold their own against the giants. "Hey," small players told their friends, "I made the basketball team." It didn't matter how short or feathery their teammates were. They were on a *team*!

Meanwhile, the teams that won championships were getting taller and taller. By 1962, when Crestmoor High School opened, boys in general were taller than those of two decades earlier, and prep athletes averaged two inches taller and twenty-five pounds heavier than their schoolmates. It was necessary, the California Interscholastic Federation decided, to adjust the exponent scale upward to accommodate the taller "boys and girls of the present decade."

Some felt it was the beginning of the end for exponent basketball. But those who favored the adjustment wanted to make sure that the new players, a little taller and heavier than their predecessors, still had an opportunity to compete against similar teams.

No matter how hard officials tried to level the basketball playing field, it was clear that competing at the lowest exponent level possible gave good athletes and the teams they played on an advantage. It meant that basketball players studied what they could do at the start of the lightweight season to lower their exponent rating. If a "B" player who had the innocence of puberty behind him could somehow find a way to step down and play "Cs" it would make him a man among boys. To achieve that there was nothing players could do to make themselves younger or shorter. Weight was the one category that could be rolled back. And in an effort to be as compact and powerful as possible, players spit in school wastebaskets, sat for hours in scalding steam baths, and starved themselves.

"Hannig is coming!" they shout. "Hannig is coming."

It is Thursday, September 12, 1968, just before the Whiz Kids' first game. The fact that the Mid-Peninsula League commissioner, Paul Hannig, is coming at two o'clock to weigh them all in is worse than an imminent attack by the Russians. Hannig is a short, officious man who carries a clipboard and who could pass for a Russian apparatchik. He is the one who will declare "nyet" if one of the players doesn't make weight. His appearance in the boys' locker room will contribute to the appearance of a Cold War invasion.

In worried anticipation of Hannig's arrival some of the Crestmoor "C" players have passed up lunch. Michael, who did a trial weigh-in that morning and found that he was still two pounds over his target weight, has spent lunchtime in a rubber sweat suit circling the balcony above the swimming pool, running and running, dodging the groups of noontime lunchers that are scattered here and there and who wonder if the quiet black kid with the bad eye has lost his mind. Lunch is for food. Lunch is for relaxation and conversation with friends. Lunch is for relief from the tedium of classroom lectures and textbooks with one sleepy paragraph after another. Lunch is not for running and sweating and exhaustion.

Two o'clock comes and Hannig is late. Michael strips and weighs himself again. Still one pound over. The team gathers around him. They rush him back into the tight rubber suit, turn one of the showers to "hot," and have him sit on a stool in the shower. He soon disappears in a cloud of steam.

The team stands outside the cloud, peering into it. After five minutes without a word from the steam cloud, they shout, "Michael, are you okay?"

Yes, he's okay.

"Hannig's still not here. We'll tell you when he gets here."

"Okay."

"Hang in there. We'll get you something good to eat after the weigh-in."

The team waits anxiously outside the steam cloud as Michael tries to lose that last critical pound. Hidden in the cloud, he is the embodiment of the "invisible man" of black life in white America: there but not there, somewhere but nowhere. The team's concern for him contains none of the superficial attention that had been paid to him when he was no more than a kid picking cotton in Oklahoma. Nor is their concern a reflection of the fact that even if they can't see him, it is his presence that will determine their basketball fortunes. They are concerned for him because he is so likeable. He quietly returns the affection because he genuinely appreciates the company of teammates who can make him laugh, defend him against racist brutes on bus rides, and most of all, he likes them because they love to play basketball as much as he does.

"What do you want?" they shout into the cloud of steam.

"We'll get you a banana split when this is over!"

Hannig finally arrives with his clipboard and a ruler he

uses to make sure nobody bends his knees when his height is recorded. Michael comes out of the steam cloud and strips out of the rubber suit. He joins his naked teammates, who are all crowded into a small team room with nothing but benches, one bank of lockers, and the scale.

They are all uncomfortable, not just because the room is small and the scale stands in one corner like an ominous guillotine. They are uncomfortable because among them are naked boys who don't have pubic hair yet, side by side with seniors who shave daily and are old enough to go to war.

As each naked prospect steps onto the scale, Hannig cracks them in their knees with his ruler to make sure they are standing straight. One by one the players step onto the scale. Two of the ten players don't make it. They are too tall, or too old, or just a pound or two too heavy. It leaves me a short roster of only eight players.

Sorry, Hannig says, the scale doesn't lie.

It only serves to increase the tension over target weights.

The Professor and Suitcase and Jack Armstrong and Salt are measured and weighed. Then they step off the scale, relieved to have made their target weight.

But nobody celebrates or trades high fives and the room remains deadly quiet because Michael is the last to be measured. He is wobbly as he steps on the scale. He has dried himself of the sweat and mist of the steam bath, to make sure the last fluid ounce of weight has been removed. Still, in the bright light of the team room his body shines like black marble statuary.

I look at a school registration card and recite Michael's age: sixteen years, ten months.

Hannig writes it down on a roster on his clipboard. No surprises there.

Then Hannig slides the steel measuring rod down so that it rests on Michael's level head. He pushes the rod into

Michael's thick head of hair, to make sure that his hair doesn't make him taller than he is.

Hannig peers at the numbers on the sliding rod—five feet eight inches. Hannig writes down the figure. No surprises there either.

Finally, Hannig slides the weight along the horizontal track of the balance. As he gets closer and closer to what everybody knows is Michael's target weight, he gently taps the sliding balance with his index finger. Tap, tap, tap.

Everyone in the room, including me, the players, even the team's manager, crowds around the scale and watches closely.

Tap, tap, tap.

Michael has his eyes closed, as if his vision, however partial it is, weighs something.

The balance finally rises a little, hovers, then hangs.

Hannig leans close to read the weight. He writes the figure on his clipboard.

The entire team can see that the balance has come to rest exactly on Michael's target weight. Not a pound of flesh to spare. But he still has his eyes closed. He steps off the scale, his head hung more than usual.

"What's wrong?" I ask him.

"I don't think I made it."

"You made it."

He shakes his head. "I don't think I made it."

"You made it. You're eligible."

It finally sinks in and Michael smiles. He's made it! He's made it!

"You made it!" I repeat. "That steam bath took off the last pound."

It is still dead quiet in the team room. The tension has been so thick and palpable that it can't be dissipated in an instant.

It is the team's manager, a bony, unathletic but witty senior, *who relieves the tension. His name is Edward Sessler, and he is the same student who can break up Michael with awkward, flailing jump shot imitations. He is the same student who once wanted something to read at halftime of a lopsided Crestmoor defeat.*

Now he looks at me, in whose English class he has read The Merchant of Venice, *Shakespeare's story of a stone-hearted Jew named Shylock. Shylock loans money to the hero of Shakespeare's tale on the condition that he can cut out a pound of flesh from the hero if he forfeits on the loan. "I will have it!" Shylock demands the pound of flesh when the hero forfeits. "I will have it!"*

Edward Sessler, himself a Jew, smiles at me now. "I guess I won't have to carve a pound of flesh out of Michael," he says.

His mother had survived both Auschwitz and Buchenwald, where she ate potato and carrot peelings to survive. By the time she was rescued by the Russian army, she weighed just seventy-five pounds and couldn't walk. She never talked about Auschwitz or Buchenwald with her children. It wasn't until a teacher recognized the tattoo on her arm at Back-to-School Night that she was asked to speak to students, including Edward and his sister. Listening to their mother's story, they both cried despite their mother's attempt to minimize the horror. "The worst thing that ever happened to me," she said in a quiet voice to a packed classroom, "was the loss of my husband."

The death of his father had also temporarily crippled Edward. "Edward's father has been dying of cancer," his counselor had written to his teachers. "They expect him to live only another week or two. Edward is probably not functioning in his usual manner."

That "usual manner" was wit, occasional comic imitations, and nonstop talking with perfect diction. But now he fell into a silence that reflected his grief over the death of his father. It seemed to foreshadow his own death, and one day not long after his father died he sat in the death seat of a friend's car after it went off the road and rolled down a cliff. "Now me!" he had shouted.

It was months before he was back to himself again, cracking jokes with an earnest, deadpan face. He got a job working weekends for Giants games at Candlestick Park, walking up and down the aisles shouting, "Hot dawwwwwwgs, peeeeee-nuts!" But he had larger ambitions in life, one of which was to express his wit and his observations about life. He wrote a column called "Splinters from the Bench" in the *Crest*, the school's student newspaper. The smell of hot dogs, mustard, and peanuts, he wrote, "cuts like a knife from the nostrils to the abdomen." It served to remind his classmates that the death of his father hadn't so numbed him that his senses had been dulled.

He took to wearing a denim sport coat and striped white shirt over a turtleneck. Occasionally he even sported a debonair ascot. It gave him the look of a preppie. But he joked that he looked like the poet William Butler Yeats's "tattered coat upon a stick." He was skinny and short and couldn't run, jump, or shoot a basketball. He made no attempt to disguise the fact that he was an athletic klutz whose lot in life was to ride the bench of every team he tried out for. Still, he was a "true cage buff" who had suffered through every losing season of basketball at Crestmoor.

In his newspaper column he spoke his own mind on school issues. He attacked coaches who insisted on silence on the busses headed for football games. He blasted a coach from crosstown rival Capuchino for pulling his team off the court in a snit over the officiating. He wrote that those who sneered at the Crestmoor "Hilltoppers" because they were a new school were troglodytes.

He had a rich, made-for-radio voice with perfect diction.

One day I told him, "You remind me of Edward R. Murrow."

"Who is he?"

"He was a golden-voiced World War II radio announcer who gave his crackly shortwave radio reports from a rooftop in London. He always started his dramatic reports with 'This is London calling.' He was a chain smoker—"

"Coach, I don't smoke. Why do I remind you of *him*?"

"—and he was a hard-hitting journalist just like you. He took on Senator McCarthy in the fifties and destroyed him. You've got all the élan and investigative grit of Edward R. Murrow. From now on, as far as I'm concerned, that's who you'll be."

He nodded and smiled, indicating he accepted my nickname for him. "I guess I should meet him, if I'm his double."

"Edward R. Murrow is dead."

"Well, then, I sure as hell don't want to meet him."

On the strength of his writing talents, Crestmoor's Edward R. Murrow got a job as a stringer for several Peninsula newspapers. Whatever readers outside the immediate community of Crestmoor High knew about the school's athletic program, it came from Edward's typewriter.

By his junior year he was editor of the *Crest*. That spring Martin Luther King Jr. was assassinated. The next morning, while half the school mourned quietly and the other half shook their fists and vowed an end to racism, the *Crest* staff worked feverishly to put out a special edition of the paper celebrating King's message of nonviolence.

Their plan was to distribute the special edition at a noontime panel presentation to discuss racism in America. When the school's principal got word of their plans, he went straight to the *Crest* faculty advisor, a five-foot-five-inch stick of journalistic dynamite named Sam Goldman, who had also spent his athletic life sitting on benches.

"Don't you know what's going to happen?" the principal warned Goldman about the panel presentation.

"Nothing ever happens at Crestmoor," Goldman answered, "except now and then a kid has his lunch stolen."

The principal wasn't amused. "There could be turmoil . . . upheaval."

Goldman nodded. "I'll make you a deal," he said.

The principal waited for Goldman to explain.

"How many kids do we have on campus?" Goldman asked.

"About fifteen hundred."

"How many black kids?"

"Two."

"Right," Goldman said. "Michael Thompson and one of the foster girls that lives with his family."

The principal nodded.

"I'll guarantee," Goldman said, "that those two kids don't riot, if you'll guarantee that the other fifteen hundred don't."

The principal laughed and the panel presentation went on as scheduled in a multipurpose room packed with students. The *Crest* staff asked Michael Thompson to be one of the four panelists. But he declined on the grounds that he was not comfortable speaking to large groups. Or even small ones, for that matter. Instead, Goldman and the *Crest* staff picked four other student speakers, one of whom was Edward Sessler. "Martin Luther King was a restraint on the powder keg of civil disorder," he said without his characteristic wit or self-effacing modesty. King's assassination had "shortened the fuse that threatens to plunge this nation into a bloodbath."

It stood as a warning of cataclysms to come, if not across a racially unsettled America then in some way in all-white San Bruno, or even closer to home, at Crestmoor High School.

SEVEN

Rene and Firp

The weigh-in is over and eight of them sit in the same small team room now, only fifteen minutes to go until tip-off for a nonconference game against South San Francisco High. They are wearing the same gold-and-blue uniforms the varsity players wear. They are all too small to fill the uniforms. Pants bunch at the belt and jerseys hang to their knees before they tuck them in. But for the first time in Crestmoor history I have passed out brand-new satin warm-up jackets tailored to fit lightweight players, and all of them sit ramrod stiff with pride.

The Falcons know they are a good team, but just how *good they are is not clear, especially to Michael. He knows that they have spent two good weeks in practice, racing up and down the floor while I studied my ten-second watch. But with only eight players, putting together a second five for a scrimmage has been difficult. Edward R. Murrow has been called in to suit up and join the second team. On several occasions even I take the floor to complete the second team. But I tire quickly and complain to Michael and the Whiz Kids, "I can't keep up with you guys." So they all know that they have yet to face any real challenge in a full-court game. South San Francisco, they think, will be that challenge.*

"Okay. Listen up," I say. "You know what to do." I

explain that Suitcase and Salt are to look deep for the Professor on every rebound or possession. If the Professor isn't open, they are to look for Michael or Jack Armstrong. "If we have to set up—," I add and then stop. I am referring to the occasional need after time-outs or inbound plays to run a set play because the fast break opportunities are foreclosed.

"If we have to set up," I repeat, "it should come about as often as a solar eclipse. I'm calling it our Solar Eclipse play."

They are too nervous to even smile.

"If you do have to run our Solar Eclipse play, you know what to do."

I do not need to explain that it is a simple play that demands quick execution and is intended to get Jack Armstrong free for a shot.

"If they press us, you also know what to do." I pause. "It's just what we want them to do. Press us. It opens up everything for us. We'll get a shot that much quicker."

I pause to run my eyes along the row of the eight proud, stiff players. "I know you're good. You know you're good. But nobody else will think any basketball team from Crestmoor is any good. That will give you an advantage the first few games, until word gets around what you can do. But I don't want you to get cocky. South City may not have finesse. They may not be able to shoot like you can. But they come from a community of hard-working boilermakers and clock punchers."

It is a reference to the white rock sign on the side of the high hill above South San Francisco. "South San Francisco," it reads. "The Industrial City."

"They're damn proud of what they can do," I finish. "So stay awake. Or they'll hammer you into the ground."

Instead the Whiz Kids hammer South City. The score is lopsided. Michael scores 23 points, most of them after dribbling the full length of the floor, weaving and spinning past one defender after another. Jack Armstrong scores 17 points. The entire team plays such relentless man-to-man defense that the South City players turn frantic and throw wild passes when they can't find anybody to pass too.

Edward R. Murrow sits next to me on the bench keeping a plus-and-minus chart at my direction for each player's defensive performance. In the locker room afterward Michael does not celebrate his scoring performance. He only wants to know, "What's the minus-six for on defense?"

The following Tuesday they played their second game, this time against El Camino High in South City. "The El Camino coach is one of the great basketball minds in the country," I say. "We'll be up against it."

The coach's name was Rene Herrerias, who for nearly a decade had coached the University of California. Herrerias was tiny, a product of San Francisco lightweight basketball. For four years he had played at St. Ignatius High in the City. He was so small—as a freshman just five feet and one hundred pounds—that he never once entertained the thought that he would one day play basketball with the big boys. Instead, in the 1940s he developed a quick shot off his hip and a lightning-quick first step that left defenders wondering where he had disappeared to. By his senior year he was an All-League player on one of the lightweight teams, but he still didn't think there were opportunities in college basketball for little men like himself.

After he got out of the navy and entered the University of San Francisco as a freshman, he was encouraged to try out for the USF varsity team. He still hadn't grown much and he was immediately cut.

He tried out again as a sophomore and this time made the team. At first he played very little and at halftime of a game against Creighton in Nebraska, he remained on the court to work on his shot.

"Who is that midget?" fans wondered.

Halfway into the season it was no longer a mystery. His USF coach, Pete Newell, who would one day be recognized as one of the coaching gurus of basketball, changed to an offense that had a role for small men like Herrerias, who could shoot, spot the open man for a pass, or steal the ball from clumsy, big players and be gone down the floor in a split second.

By 1949, on the strength of a six-foot-eight-inch Goliath named Don Lofgren and a still-tiny Rene Herrerias, USF received an invitation to the National Invitational Tournament in Madison Square Garden. In the final game against Loyola, which USF won by 1 point, Rene Herrerias was the sweetheart of the tournament, a human "buzz saw who was dashing everywhere." Afterward, his picture appeared on the cover of *Sport* magazine with Don Lofgren towering over him.

Six years later, after he had gone to the University of California, Newell picked Herrerias as his assistant. Then Newell left coaching to become athletic director at Cal, and the midget who had once been an unknown figure was the new head coach at the University of California.

In 1967 the challenge of coaching young university athletes who could be self-indulgent and demanding proved discouraging and Herrerias stepped down. He took a job teaching at El Camino High in South City. He loved history and in a high school classroom his passion for it was infectious. He also still loved basketball, and the human buzz saw who had been one of the sweethearts of the basketball world now stood as a likely nemesis for the Crestmoor Falcons.

"Play hard," Herrerias tells his players before the game. "Do the best you can. If we win, we win."

They play a deliberate, patterned game with ingenious double screens and pinpoint passing. But it is another lopsided

victory for the Falcons. Again and again the Professor finds
himself wide open with the ball on the baseline. He scores
18 points. Michael also scores 18 points. But in the locker
room he again refuses to celebrate, this time because he has
missed so many free throws.
  "Don't worry about it," I tell him. "We'll work on it."

Michael continued to fret over his inability to shoot free
throws. The Professor told him, "Why don't you shoot a
jump shot at the free-throw line. Your jump shot is deadly."

He experimented with it but the shot failed him. He became
even more depressed. So one day during the shootaround I
took him to one of the main baskets. "Nobody can tell you
how to shoot free throws," I said. "Good athletes like you
just watch and learn."

Michael looked skeptical.

"Look, Michael, I'm a pretty good free-throw shooter,"
I said. "But I don't have any idea how I got to be."

Michael smiled.

"So let's do this. I'm gonna shoot free throws. You stand
just outside the free-throw circle and watch. That's all you
do is watch. You understand?"

He nodded.

"Okay. Give me the ball."

Michael handed me the ball and I designated a player to
stand under the net and bounce the ball back to me after
every free throw. I began shooting. For the first few free
throws, I missed occasionally. Then I began a streak. Eight,
ten, twenty, twenty-five in a row. One after the other, as
quickly as the ball came out of the net and it was bounced
back to me, I continued shooting. Thirty, forty, fifty in a row.
Some of the players shooting around spotted what was
happening and gathered beside Michael to watch. Sixty,
seventy, eighty, ninety. At one hundred they whooped. Michael

was the only one who didn't. He was still watching closely, noting my execution for each free throw at some level of concentration that was so deep he seemed in a trance.

One-ten, one-twenty, one-thirty.

The entire team gathered now. They were all counting: One-thirty-one.

The ball came right back to me.

One-thirty-two.

A hush fell in the gym.

One-thirty-three.

I missed at one-thirty-four. There was a collective groan from the players. Then they cheered. I had made 133 free throws in a row. But Michael pushed me aside.

"Okay," he said. "Let me try."

His head was cocked. He held the ball over his right shoulder. At the end of the shot his right arm remained extended, as if it was the gun barrel he had sighted along to hit the target.

He had done nothing different that I could spot. It was the same free-throw technique that led him to all of his misses. The ball traveled exactly the same trajectory as all his other shots and ripped the net.

He continued to shoot, eleven in a row. Afterward he quietly insisted, "I'm not gonna miss, from here on."

It was confidence that was uncharacteristic for such a shy creature who always seemed to be hanging his head in shame. For what? For missing free throws? For being half blind? For being the only black kid in school? For not wanting any part of cotton picking or living in a black enclave where defeat was so long-standing and corrosive that the glassy-eyed young victims stood in groups on street corners with a bottle of beer and loud music to bring on forgetfulness?

The seven schools in the San Mateo High School District make

up the Mid-Peninsula Athletic League. The Falcons open their
MPL *play against their crosstown rivals, the Capuchino Mustangs. Cap is a school with mystique and athletic tradition.
In the 1950s the Mustangs had won* MPL *championships in
football, basketball, baseball, and track. The huge Cap marching band, in bright green-and-gold uniforms with epaulettes
and tasseled hats, with snare drums and tubas and slide trombones, marched and played at JFK's inauguration.*

*Meanwhile, Crestmoor is the school on the hill that can't
get its pep song in the right key. Crestmoor is the school of
defeat and wind. It is the school that some San Bruno kids
refuse to be a part of, so they create false addresses within
Capuchino's boundaries so that they can attend a "good"
school.*

*It is an attitude that makes the Capuchino Mustangs the
mortal enemies of Crestmoor, whether the Falcon's high-flying "C" team can beat them or not. But the Falcons coast
to a third lopsided victory, nearly doubling Capuchino's score.
Suitcase, who loves the Capuchino gym because it is the site
of his early basketball days as a new immigrant in San Bruno,
scores 13 points. Jack Armstrong scores repeatedly with his
"float move" that takes him through Capuchino defenders
who swat and slash at him. Michael comes flying in from
half court to grab a long rebound and then slinks and spins
his way through defenders until he reaches the basket and
puts up a soft layup. The three substitutes on the bench and
I all leap to our feet and make fists. Yeah! Yeah! Yeah! Take
that, you smug Mustangs!*

*Mills High School is next. It is a carbon copy of Crestmoor,
with its I-beam style of architectural Brutalism and an all-white community. When the Whiz Kids get off the bus and
head for the locker room for visiting teams, Michael is wearing
his fedora, as if he were barrel-bellied, rip-roaring Fats Waller
instead of a tiny rattlebones.*

"What's with the hat?" one of his teammates asks him.
"My father likes hats," he says.
The coach of the Mills Vikings meets the Falcons in front
of the gym and ushers them to their locker room. "We're not
very good," he tells me. Then he turns to Michael and the
Whiz Kids. "Good luck," he says and heads for his own
locker room.

His name was Frank Firpo and he was at home in the company of wee people. It hadn't started out that way. As a kid in San Francisco, looking for distinction on a basketball court, he had shot up to five feet nine inches in elementary school. He played center on his eighth-grade team, confident that one day if he kept growing he would be one of those rangy players that dominated the game.

But five feet nine inches was as tall as he would get, and the teammates who had once scrambled around beneath him hung the nickname Firp on him. It was a nickname as short as he was. "Hey, little man," those friends said, "we passed you up." At St. Ignatius High School his coach was a tiny, fledgling teacher named Rene Herrerias, who knew what it took for little men to succeed. "You're gonna have to learn defensive skills," Herrerias told him. "You're gonna have to learn to dribble and handle the ball."

He practiced all by himself, day and night, at an outdoor court in the avenues in San Francisco, wearing a heavy jacket when the fog rolled in. By the time he was a senior at St. Ignatius he was the little varsity player whose hustle electrified fans. He carried that same enthusiasm into coaching. He loved fast-break basketball and, like me, would blow his whistle in practice to stop play if the pace was too slow or somebody had passed up a good shot. During a game he was excitable and fiery, popping up and down on the bench to spark his players, whether they were any good or not.

The Mills gym is the smallest in the MPL, a true "cracker box" in which the sound of the buzzer to start the game reverberates like a foghorn. There are only a handful of people in the bleachers and they don't even shout or cheer.

Even before the end of the first quarter, the Falcons have doubled the Vikings' score. But in the fourth quarter, Michael fouls out.

One of the three possible substitutes for Michael is a junior whose pithy name, Hubbs, perfectly captures how small he is. At five feet two inches he is the shortest member of the team. In scrimmages he seldom scores, but he is quick and eager and he reports to the scorer's bench.

In the fourth quarter Suitcase throws a long bullet pass to the Professor, who fumbles with the ball to get it under control before he heads for the basket. But defenders have retreated to stop him, so he slices to the left side of the basket, stops, and takes his favorite jump shot. It skips off the glass, swirls around the rim, and flies straight out.

Suitcase has been racing down the floor after his long pass, and he leaps and grabs the rebound.

Edward R. Murrow and I come to our feet together. "Yeah!" we growl, celebrating the bantam Latvian who plays as if he were seven feet tall.

Still holding the ball, Suitcase lands on one foot with a crunch that sounds like he has stepped on a box of cornflakes. He collapses to the floor and grabs his ankle. The ball trickles out of bounds.

They take Suitcase to the hospital for X-rays. I stand on the floor looking down my short bench of only two possible substitutes. One of the possible substitutes for the injured Suitcase is a five-feet-five-inch senior named David Esposto. Despite his size, however, he is a ferocious rebounder in practice. One of my favorite conditioning drills is to throw a spinning ball high in the air and then have the team shuffle

back and forth in a defensive crouch until the ball stops
bouncing or rolling. If anybody loafs or tires, I throw the
ball up again. It is grueling and maddening. But David Esposto
always smiles broadly as he shuffles back and forth, back
and forth. Either he loves the pain, I decide, or he is superbly
conditioned.

"Esposto," I call now and point to him.

He jumps up and rips off his satin warm-up jacket. Facing
me, he is not smiling and instead shakes with nervousness.
He knows he is not the same caliber of player as Michael
and Jack Armstrong and the Professor, and he does not want
to make a single mistake that will cost the team a victory

I put my hand on his bony shoulder. "Relax," I say. "This
is only a game."

He trots onto the floor and responds with his typically
aggressive rebounding. He is fouled again and again by Vikings
who try to tear the ball from his grip. In the dead quiet he
makes one free throw after another. He is soon smiling again.
The Falcons roll to another easy victory.

The game ended with only one eligible substitute sitting on
the bench beside me. I wondered if I shouldn't have Edward
R. Murrow put on Suitcase's uniform just in case. The next
day I held a team meeting to discuss who they could get to
bolster their roster.

"I know who we can get," the Professor offered.

"Who?" I wondered. I did not want a miniature Tongan
who couldn't dribble and might puncture the ball.

"We can get Darrell Hirashima," the Professor said. "I
realize he's short—"

Everybody laughed. Who on the team wasn't short?

The Professor plunged ahead. "But if we wind up having
to play shorthanded, he's worth two men on defense."

Most of the stories about playing shorthanded in basketball

were apocryphal. But they were accepted because tales of shorthanded basketball underdogs, with only four or three players battling against overwhelming odds, were thrilling. Most of the stories came out of small, rural communities with teams that practiced in barns and could barely scrape together five players for the high school team.

Having no substitutes at all and winding up having to play shorthanded was an eventuality I did not look forward to. However effortlessly the Falcons had coasted to four straight victories, it would have been foolish to think they could win shorthanded against a good team, and I commissioned the Professor and Jack Armstrong to recruit tiny Darrell Hirashima.

He was the oldest of six kids, all born in San Francisco to Hiroshi and Toki Hirashima. As a young, single woman Toki had been one of the 110,000 Japanese Americans interned during the hysteria of World War II. Back east, Darrell's father had escaped the same fate by convincing military authorities that he was Chinese. After the war Hiroshi had come to California bearing the nickname Blackie. He also had a mysterious past that he had left behind him in favor of respectability in the San Francisco produce business.

The family was among the first Asian families in San Bruno. His friends tried to nickname Darrell "Fuji," emphasizing his Japanese heritage. But he politely objected. He was as American as apple pie. He loved the Rolling Stones. He loved to play tackle football, despite the fact that some of his bigger friends would have crushed him if he hadn't been as quick and strong as they were. He loved to go fishing in the bay with his father, then filet the catch. He had a white girlfriend named Theresa who looked as vibrant as the models who appeared in *Look* magazine advertisements drinking Coca-Cola.

"I prefer to be called Darrell," he told his friends.

When he entered Crestmoor in 1966 he weighed ninety-six pounds and was just five feet tall. He had a baby face, a wide-eyed innocence, and the sweet disposition of a house cat. But when he stepped onto a wrestling mat he was like a stalking lion in a tense crouch. As a lightweight wrestler nobody could beat him. He was soon recognized anywhere on campus, not just because he was friendly and a popular athlete but because he and his wrestling teammates shaved their heads to look like monks.

The Professor was the first to approach him about joining the "C" team. "You're quick," the Professor told him. "We need another good athlete."

Darrell explained that he was first and foremost a wrestler. He was concerned about hurting an ankle in basketball and forfeiting his wrestling season.

Jack Armstrong and Salt also coaxed him. The team was on its way to a championship, they said. "We're not counting on you to come in and score all the time. But we need you." On the bench. Just in case.

Darrell Hirashima now became the smallest member of the team. David Esposto continued to fill in for Suitcase, creating the confusion of three Daves on the starting five.

Edward R. Murrow reminded me that there were nicknames for everybody but Michael. "You've got Suitcase, Jack Armstrong, the Professor, and Salt," he said. "You need a nickname for David Esposto."

"I can't think of one," I said. "What do you suggest?"

"How about Dago?"

I shook my head.

"Why not?"

"What if people called you Jew-boy. Or kike?"

"They do."

"How do you like it when they do?"

He smiled before he explained. "Coach, my ancestors were *kikes*. Many of them died in concentration camps. My mother was one of the few to survive. Auschwitz. She survived Auschwitz! So *kike* doesn't bother me. Or *Jew-boy* or *sheenie* or *yid*. They can call me anything they want. As long as they don't put me in a gas chamber."

EIGHT

Bob and Red

The Falcons were averaging almost 70 points a game. They had won three straight league games by lopsided scores. Their next game was against Burlingame High, the only other undefeated team in the league. But the Panthers had a reputation of being "pussycats," of being overindulged rich kids whose lives were full of Ivy League expectations and a sense of entitlement. It was the school for kids with fancy cars and expensive clothes. It was the school for kids who went to basketball camps and had private tutors for math. It was the school that parents flocked to on Back-to-School Night to oversee the education of their children.

I knew that the Burlingame Panthers' reputation as a school for "pussycats" was not legitimate. Their teachers were friendly but demanding. Their students were smart. Their athletes were talented and dedicated. Their coaches knew how to motivate young athletes. Whatever high-flying confidence the Falcons had, I knew it was unwarranted.

"You guys have a target on your backs," I tell my undefeated Falcons on the bus to the game. "Every team we play is gonna step it up against us. I know you will give it 100 percent. But Burlingame will give it 150 percent. That means you have to step it up. They may press us. It shouldn't bother us. It's just what we want."

Salt enters the glass doors to the Burlingame gym, which has a box office and championship pennants that hang from the ceiling like read-and-white stalactites and cover the school's long history. Salt has played well in the gym before and he tells himself, "Man, I like playing here." He is certain that he is going to have a good game.

I tape Suitcase's injured ankle and he starts the game. But he is without his usual rebounding effectiveness. Whatever Michael learned watching me shoot free throws has worn off and he misses repeatedly. Whenever the Falcons get the ball the Panthers retreat so fast on defense that the Professor can't get a shot. The open floor that Jack Armstrong needs to weave his way through defenders until he's close enough to float to the basket—that is also gone. Only Salt seems undisturbed by Burlingame's play and he knocks Panther players aside to snag rebounds, then put the ball back in the basket.

At the end of the first quarter, the Panthers lead by 1 point. It is the first game in which the Falcons haven't raced to a huge early lead. In the brief huddle I say nothing that would suggest I am worried. But at the end of the half the Falcons lead by just 1 point. Only the play of Salt and the defense of Jack Armstrong have kept them in the game.

At halftime I tell them, "I told you we'd have to play harder."

In the third quarter they do, and they start the fourth quarter with a 6-point lead. It is the beginning, I think, of another rout.

I am wrong.

The Panthers' coach was Bob Milano. Milano grew up in Oakland playing sandlot baseball. In high school he also played basketball, but on the court he was only a sparrow among storks. His coaches told him, "You're wasting your time playing basketball."

He concentrated then on baseball. As soon as he graduated from high school the Chicago Cubs offered him a contract. But his father insisted that he go to college first. The little catcher who crouched behind home plate like a "fireplug" was quickly recruited by the University of California. "You get anything lower than a C," his father told him, "no baseball."

He rode the streetcar every day to the university campus, kept up good grades, and distinguished himself as an All-Pac-10 catcher. Professional baseball was again a possibility. But he was recruited to be a teacher at Burlingame High School. That fall of 1968 was his first year coaching lightweight basketball. He understood from his own athletic career how his "sawed-off midgets," as he called them, could use quickness and deception to get the most out of their tiny bodies. But he readily admitted that he was not an expert on basketball strategies. What he didn't know, he assured his players, he would ask "Coach B."

Coach B was Frank Bettendorf, Burlingame's varsity basketball coach. As a freshman at Arcata High School in northern California, he was four feet eleven inches and weighed ninety pounds. He had flaming-red hair that earned him the nickname Red, but he wore an athletic jacket with the name "Whitey" stitched on it, in honor of a basketball player he admired. He studied drama at UCLA. At Burlingame he taught drama and coached varsity basketball. The two roles meant a continuation of the duality of his Red and Whitey nicknames. The red half of him could discuss the rigid certainties of basketball tactics at the same time that his white half loved the ambiguities of drama and literature.

Bob Milano brings inspiration and intensity to his players. Red Bettendorf, who sits writing on a clipboard in a row behind Milano and his Panthers, is a brilliant student of basketball tactics. Together the two men are a potent coaching force.

"Press them," Red Bettendorf says before the fourth quarter starts. "You gotta stop their first pass. You can't let 'em run."

He tells Milano to put in a substitute for a Burlingame player who is bent over with fatigue in the huddle and grabbing his shorts.

Now it is Milano's turn. "Your feet are lazy," he tells his team. "I don't want to see anybody with his head down." The buzzer sounds to resume play. "Okay," he says, "let's go."

The Burlingame press doesn't seem to work. The Falcons open up an 11-point lead. I think another rout is in the making.

Again I am wrong.

Burlingame begins to intercept passes and force turnovers. The margin narrows: 8 points, 7 points, 6 points. The Panthers' bench is on its feet. The Panthers rebound a missed Falcons' shot and fly down the floor. The score continues to narrow: 4 points, 3 points, 2 points, tie game.

The last thirty seconds are a frantic free-for-all of missed shots, picked off passes, and racing up and down the floor. The game has become a basketball street fight. The mighty Falcons have lost their composure and become frenetic failures.

With ten seconds to go Michael rebounds a missed Burlingame shot and doesn't even look down the floor for the Professor or Jack Armstrong. He breaks away from the Burlingame rebounder who is trying to trap him with the ball. To escape he pushes one long dribble and then heads down the floor. He catches up with the dribble and begins dodging and weaving his way through Burlingame defenders, who are all backpedaling fast. He beats the first and second defender easily, but the remaining defender is also backing up fast and is crouched low.

As Michael approaches the basket, he does not seem to be closing space on the defender. His only hope for getting a clear shot is to leap into the air. But just before Michael is airborne the Burlingame player sets his feet and waits for Michael to crash into him.

In the air Michael crooks himself so that the bottom half of his body slides right by the Burlingame defender. He holds the ball high above the defender's head as he soars over the arms reaching up for him.

The eventual release of the ball from his right hand is more a soft shoveling of the ball than a shot. It is in the air when the buzzer sounds.

The basket is good. But I am afraid to look at the scoreboard. When I do I can't believe the final score: Falcons 47, Panthers 45.

San Bruno was where well-behaved boys with spit-licked hair sat like figures in a Norman Rockwell painting while they folded the papers for their newspaper routes and secretly listened to the music of the Doors. San Bruno meant going to school and getting a job.

It wasn't much different anywhere else on the Peninsula, with shopping malls and ticky-tacky homes. But just fifteen miles away the Haight was a glow in the sky with music so new and strange that listeners could forget everything. The Haight was freedom and hairy wild wonders. For San Bruno teenagers it was like going to the zoo.

Haight heretics shouted about how boring and circumscribed life in the suburbs was compared to experiencing the infinite possibilities of the Haight. Life in the suburbs, the new rebels complained, meant not moving, not creating. They argued that the social patterns of life had isolated humans from their consciousness. Consciousness needed to be expanded, not shrunk. Consciousness needed to replace numbness and sleepwalking. A spirited life meant merry pranksters driving around the country in the cuckoo's nest of a psychedelic bus promoting freedom from parental overlords and the accepted order of things.

It was a movement that took hold. By 1966 there were over two hundred rock bands in the Bay Area, many of them centered in the Haight. "There's no limit," rock evangelists predicted, "to how big this thing can get." Suddenly youth had its own culture, its own rules. The new rules were furious, howling music and spontaneity. The advocates of the new consciousness held rallies in the Panhandle and a meadow of Golden Gate Park to urge freedom of body and the pursuit of joy. Followers came to the rallies with beads and flags and banners. They wore colorful costumes and they brought photos of saints and gurus who had once been oracles. They burned incense and smoked so much dope that clouds of scud hung over the meadow.

For San Bruno kids the marijuana was okay, despite teachers who lectured to them that reefers led to madness, sex, and death. But LSD trips into the infinite were frightening. And the very tether that kept them fastened to the predictability of San Bruno, from street games like "over-the-line" to tardy bells at school, was what kept them from falling into the unknown perils of the Haight.

Instead, they cruised the Haight at night like rubberneckers looking to buy up marijuana. Distraught parents who thought of the Haight as a psychedelic Sodom caught their daughters trying to smoke marijuana in the bushes of San Bruno parks and told them, "I wish you were pregnant instead of this." When those San Bruno teenagers couldn't get to the Haight, dances in the Crestmoor girls' gym were meant to be knockoffs of Haight spontaneity. The whole gym shook with the pounding music, while overhead projectors threw images on the gym walls that were made to dance and shiver by students shaking huge woks filled with colored oil and water. It was as if they were panning for gold.

One of the first Crestmoor students to answer the call of the Haight was Greg Shaw, who at fifteen years old spent whatever time he wasn't in school sequestered in his room listening to the new music and drawing maps of an imaginary land. "My world is inside the confines of my bedroom," he said. His bedroom was an "oasis of security in a world of chaos." The bored boy from San Bruno was soon in the Haight, editing and peddling ten-cent copies of the *Mojo Navigator*, one of the Haight's first underground magazines with rock-and-roll news. The magazine carried interviews with Janis Joplin and colorful broadside inserts for the Grateful Dead, who maintained that "in the land of the dark, the ship of the sun is driven by the grateful dead." The land of the dark, it was assumed, was suburban America and especially the San Bruno that Greg Shaw had fled. The grateful dead were those benumbed suburbanites for whom the ship of the sun was the Haight.

Crestmoor's Whiz Kids weren't far behind Greg Shaw in seeking the glow of the Haight. On Thursday, October 3, the Falcons enjoyed a bye and a weekend off from basketball, and several of them headed for the Haight. It had become a ritual that at first had meant walking north on the El Camino to Mission Street in Daly City, then using money from paper routes to take a bus to the Haight. When they were old enough to drive they piled into one car and headed for San Francisco and concerts at the Fillmore and the Avalon. In an abandoned and restored firehouse they gawked at the weird spectacle of people on one side of the station listening to electric music, while stoned girls in flowery muumuus on the other side watched black-and-white industrial training films as if they were the movie *King Kong*. In Victorian mansions, with a different band every week, they were told that sports were just an extension of corporate life. Kids from the suburbs with greasy flattops, wondering if the bands knew any "Negro tunes"—they were the oddballs. The Haight apostles urged them to "tune in, drop out." When the Whiz Kids drove home in the late hours it was to the comfortable tedium of San Bruno life and the excitement of basketball.

NINE

Noah

San Mateo High School opened in 1902 in a two-story cottage with three teachers and fourteen students. The founders couldn't agree on whether the mascot should be a bear or a cat. They settled on "Bearcat," even if there wasn't such an animal, and they adopted the orange-and-black colors of Princeton, hoping to follow in the prestigious academic and sports footsteps of the Ivy League school.

In 1927 they built a new school modeled after Henry VIII's Hampton Court, with a red-brick facade, cathedral windows, and long corridors, the hub of which was a vaulted rotunda. They also built a separate gym with a red-brick facade. They were soon calling the gym The Pit, because fans sat high up in rows of wooden benches on a balcony that looked down on a court that seemed to sit at the bottom of a hole in the ground.

In the early years the program of classes offered to students was described as a "Schedule of Recitations." With that program and a gym that was soon out of style came a reputation for being old-fashioned and hidebound. However, efforts to modernize the school were difficult. After they unscrewed the rows of desks so that students could meet in collegial circles and discuss rather than recite, the janitors who swept the rooms at night lined the desks back up with the screw holes in the floor.

In 1968 most of its students came from the city of San Mateo and a new community called Foster City, a middle-class suburb of apartments and single-family dwellings on San Francisco Bay landfill. The school also included students from the community of Hillsborough, one of the wealthiest residential areas in the United States. Finally, San Mateo High drew a small group of students from the predominantly black and Hispanic neighborhood immediately south of the San Mateo campus.

One of the first blacks to settle in San Mateo was Noah Williams, who came from a San Francisco family of noted cooks. Williams built a fourteen-room house for his family just south of San Mateo High. Then he opened Noah's Cafeteria in the downtown district of San Mateo. He came to work at 4:00 a.m. to begin preparing his trademark buffet supper of baked ham, potatoes, and fried chicken. His recipes were so secret that he worked in a locked kitchen.

"Grandpa Daddy," everyone began calling him. His restaurant became so profitable and popular with white diners in the 1920s and '30s that they had to wait in long lines to get in on Sunday nights. He began to hire black waiters and busboys, telling them, "You come to San Mateo, you'll have a good job. You'll be able to buy a home."

But the only area where the new blacks could buy a home was adjacent to the San Mateo High School campus where Noah had settled. Black families began to move into the area as if they were streaming aboard Noah's ark. Whites called the new blacks-only enclave Sugar Hill. It was where all the rich black folk lived, they said. Wednesday night became the only night that those so-called rich folks from Sugar Hill could dine at Noah's. The rest of the week Noah's good food was for whites only.

Still, black families continued to move into the area. By the 1950s what was once called Sugar Hill was referred to as Eastside, because it lay east of the railroad tracks. The inhabitants were anything but rich. But their sons played basketball all day on outdoor courts, or at night they sneaked into The Pit. When it became clear that the black community of Eastside needed a recreation facility of its own, the city fathers built a modern recreation center with a gym that had bright lights and glass backboards. The new rec center was in the heart of the Eastside community, but the hope was that it would "not be segregated in any way."

It became an exciting recreational hangout for black athletes from Eastside. Those bright lights were on day and night, illuminating full-court pickup games of five-on-five, with game winners holding the court against all opponents. Out of those nearly nonstop games came talented and tall black athletes who helped make San Mateo High into a basketball powerhouse.

The Pit began to draw packed houses for basketball games. The opposing teams came out of their locker room and up an inclined tunnel to step onto the lighted floor with bouncy cheerleaders flashing orange pom-poms and pep bands that tried to drown each other out. It didn't matter that The Pit still had thick wooden backboards and tight rims that made shots ricochet. It was like stepping onto the floor of Madison Square Garden.

By the spring of 1968 the stucco walls of the school carried pictures in latex paint of George Washington, Abraham Lincoln, Freud, Newton, FDR, Walt Whitman, Thoreau, Jack London, and eventually Martin Luther King Jr. Those giants of history seemed appropriate company for the modern, distinguished graduates of San Mateo High, including the pop icon Merv Griffin, the artist Sam Francis, the jazz musician Cal Tjader, and the actors Barry Bostwick and Kris Kristofferson.

For the nearly one hundred black students at San Mateo,

who had only the wall icon of Martin Luther King to celebrate, the impact of his assassination on Thursday, April 4, 1968, was devastating. On Friday morning after the assassination over two hundred students, most of them black, staged a sit-in in the vaulted-ceiling rotunda, just inside the school's front entrance.

The bell rang for first period. None of them moved. They shouted and sang gospel hymns. They recited the Lord's Prayer. They talked of oppression and demanded black history classes "or else." They wanted mandatory in-service training for all teachers because they didn't understand black culture. They wanted black guest speakers to be invited to classes. They wanted black cops and security guards at their dances.

Meanwhile, after King's assassination the news was that other schools on the Peninsula were experiencing student walkouts and bottle throwing. Black students refused to go to class. Gangs of angry students stopped traffic on the Bayshore Freeway. Police cars surrounded the schools. Classes were dismissed. Elsewhere the black activist Stokely Carmichael led hundreds of demonstrators in Washington. "Black people have to survive," he said. "The only way they will survive is by getting guns."

With some black leaders urging violence, the question was, what would the San Mateo High student protestors in the rotunda do?

The first person to try to intervene was a young English teacher named Barry Miller, who sported a thick pompadour of swept-back hair in the image of James Dean.

He tried to shout over the noise in the rotunda. "C'mon, guys, this isn't getting you anywhere. Go to class."

Instead the protestors marched out of the rotunda and assembled on a street corner directly across from the school. Miller followed them, pleading with them to go to class.

"We're not going to class," they insisted.

Teachers who watched from the windows of the school worried about Miller's safety. More bells rang. The campus observed five minutes of silence in memory of Dr. King. Bugles sounded a slow, melancholy taps.

Before the morning was over the crowd of protestors had grown to three hundred. They marched silently to San Mateo city hall carrying symbolic palms. In the city council chambers they listened to sympathetic remarks from councilmen, ministers, rabbis, and community leaders. In the days that followed nearly five thousand peaceful demonstrators marched from downtown San Mateo to the school's football field, where a special memorial program for Martin Luther King was held.

By October 1968, the San Mateo Rec Center had been officially renamed the Martin Luther King Center. Eldridge Cleaver, who had spent the summer delivering fiery speeches, was barred from the UC Berkeley campus after Governor Ronald Reagan received nearly four thousand letters protesting against him teaching black history. Huey Newton, the controversial black activist from Oakland, was convicted of killing an Oakland cop and sentenced to up to fifteen years in jail.

In response to the protests at San Mateo High, the school hired a black teacher to present a course in black history. The teacher of the course was a young man from back east named Ike Tribble, who came into the school like the wind. His course would, the school's newspaper reported, "help whites to better understand black contributions to American history." He had dedicated himself to correcting the stereotype of blacks as "dumb, lazy, possessed with natural rhythm, and immoral." He said he would accentuate the positives of black people. He would help whites view the black man's struggle through a black man's eyes. "This is just a start," he said. He was bright and articulate, but his abrupt, confrontational manner alienated some faculty. Yet students who complained regularly about dull lectures and boring homework praised him and his course. "When he starts to blow, baby," they said, "we're wide awake."

Meanwhile, the demonstrations were peaceful. Thirty-five black students from San Mateo High met with the city's police chief for forty-five minutes to complain that they were being observed and harassed by "unidentified white persons" who came into the black community. The police assured the protestors that it wasn't police who were doing the harassing and observing.

"If they aren't police, who are they?" the protestors wanted to know. "They could mean bodily harm."

"Whenever you are being annoyed," the chief reassured them, "I want you to call on us."

When Michael and the Whiz Kids arrived for a game at San Mateo on Tuesday, October 10, the protestors' demands hadn't gone away, but the threat of violence to achieve those demands had subsided. The major point in question now was whether or not the undefeated Falcons, as strong as they were, would be able to stave off defeat at the hands of San Mateo, whose tiny black and Asian players made them a yearly lightweight powerhouse. Could the Falcons descend into the deep netherworld of The Pit and bring home another victory?

At six feet five inches, San Mateo coach Jim Snider was the tallest coach in the Mid-Peninsula League and a giant among his colleagues and especially among his players. Snider was a product of East Bay high school basketball and the University of California. In 1966, his first year at San Mateo, he struggled to manage the demands of teaching social science and coaching basketball. He didn't leave school until after dark, carrying home a clump of student papers to be graded late into the night while his wife laundered the old sweat-soaked uniforms that were as stiff as body armor.

His "C" team went undefeated but at the end of the year he asked himself, "Do I really want to do this?"

He took a leave of absence for a year for graduate study and returned to San Mateo High in 1968, refreshed and ready to bring San Mateo its fourth-straight "C" championship. Half his players were black, among them the tiny brothers Renaldo "Bobo" Groves and his little brother Joe, who had honed their basketball skills at the nearby King Center and were among the best players in the league.

Before the game with Crestmoor Snider prepared his team to play a full-court press and an aggressive zone defense in which his players would flit back and forth like bugs. To prepare for the possibility of a close game that came down to a last-second shot, he reminded his players of his Heart Attack play, which he called for during a game by putting his fist to his heart. It was an ingenious play that the Bearcats had used only once. But the player who got the shot delivered an air ball. "I was so wide open," the player told Snider, "I got nervous."

In an old, dark team room that smells of forty years of lin-iment and sweat, I tape Suitcase's ankle. "Okay, listen up," I say to the team. I tell them that Jack Armstrong and Michael are leading the league in scoring. But the Groves brothers are right behind them. I remind Jack Armstrong that he has been assigned to guard Bobo Groves. "Shut him down!" I say.

Then I address the team. "You got soft against Burlingame. If you get that soft against the Bearcats, you're gonna get whipped. Burlingame played over their heads. The Bearcats can loaf and still be good. But you are better. You can run. When this is over they're not gonna know what hit 'em."

None of the Whiz Kids is reassured. The idiosyncrasies of The Pit have spooked them: the out-of-bounds lines are only inches from the walls of the sunken gym; the old wooden backboards with rigid rims will mean a lot of missed shots; in the afternoon light that streams in from the high windows of the gym, there are parts of the floor that seem to have spotlights on them; the scorer's bench is ten feet above the floor, so any player trying to enter the game has to shout up to the timer and wave his hands.

As the Falcons come up the ramp and onto the floor of The Pit, they are greeted by a few hoots and jeers in the nearly empty gym. In his lightweight career Michael has never played well in The Pit. The other Whiz Kids don't like the floor, the lighting, the tight rims, or the fact that fans behind the baskets can hang over that balcony and shout catcalls down on the visiting teams. It is Salt who is spooked the most. "We're gonna get our butts kicked," he thinks.

But it is another Falcon rout from the start. They have had a weekend off and have caroused in the Haight. Now they are as loose and free as the birds after which they are named. At halftime they lead by fourteen points. On the fast break Jack Armstrong pulls up twenty-five feet from the basket and buries jump shots. The Bearcats do not cover the Professor. Suitcase fires him full-court bull's-eye passes and the Professor scores six sleeper baskets. Despite the tight rims the Falcons rarely miss. When they do Salt grabs the rebounds that carom off the rims and wrestles them back in the basket. Bobo Groves can't get the ball, and when he does he can't get free to shoot.

It is only Michael who can't seem to get started. He misses seven straight shots. What throws him off his game is the taunting from the Bearcat black players.

"You think you're good!" they tell him.

"Yeah, he thinks he's All-League."

"He thinks he's baaaaad."

"Hey, Uncle Tom," they whisper to him after they position themselves next to him for free throws, "why you playin' up there in honky town?"

"These white boys wouldn't be worth shit without you."

"Wait until we meet again up at Crestmoor."

In the locker room at halftime he hangs his head.

Jack Armstrong asks him, "What's wrong?"

The Professor, who has heard the taunts, tells Michael, "It's just a game. When it's over we'll get back to our lives."

In the second half Michael finds the basket and the Falcon lead widens to 20 points. Tiny Darrell Hirashima and Hubbs, who are eager to be a part of the rout, jump up and down and wave their arms in front of the scorer's bench, trying to get the attention of the timer so they can enter the game.

The Falcons win by 30 points. There are no Heart Attack plays or last-second desperation shots.

"You put up seventy-eight shots," I tell the team in the locker room, "in twenty-eight minutes of play." I shake my head in disbelief. Then I hold up my wrist with the Actua Chronograph. "Every time we got the ball we took a shot in about eight seconds." I pause and smile. "Why were you so sluggish?"

They all laugh.

But when Edward R. Murrow puts on his best radio voice and tries to call the results in to local newspapers, they refuse to take the score. Nobody beats a Bearcat lightweight team by 30 points, they insist, and hang up.

Now I call them back. "We're an awfully good team," I say.

"Riiiiight," they say and hang up again.

Meanwhile, Michael is still hanging his head.

"What's wrong?" I ask him.

He doesn't explain.

"Michael, we won the game!"

Jack Armstrong shouts, "We stomped them!"

The Professor agrees. "We embarrassed the hell out of 'em."

Michael still doesn't smile.

"You're too hard on yourself," I tell him.

Michael lifts his head and stares at me, as if to say, *What do* you *know about hard? With "Coach" stitched in gold on your jacket, defining you gloriously, what do* you *know about being so tight and guarded about who you are and what you do that you can never relax? What do* you *know, Coach, about cutting a trail through a jungle of suspicion and racial taunts?*

When he heads for the team bus after the game Michael remembers his mother's repeated admonitions about ignoring racial taunts. But he finds a baseball bat in one of the lockers and has it in one hand as he walks quickly to the bus.

TEN

Darnell

The victory over San Mateo in The Pit should have been a sign of what racial difficulties were still to come. But the incident was quickly forgotten by everybody except Michael, who was convinced that the Bearcat players, embittered by such a lopsided defeat, would come up to Crestmoor vowing revenge and determined to do more taunting.

Meanwhile, the night of the victory was Back-to-School Night and the halls of Crestmoor were jammed with parents, among them Michael's mother, who wanted to hear from her son's teachers that he was the model citizen she expected him to be.

At the end of the night, I spoke for ten minutes in the gym to my "C" team parents about how good the team was. "They could win the championship," I said.

Doris Thompson was the first to approach me after my short presentation. "How is Michael doing?" she wanted to know.

"He's doing fine." I chose not to tell her about the taunting at San Mateo. "He's leading the league in scoring."

"Is he behaving himself?"

"Always."

"You know, some of his friends have gotten in trouble."

"Not your son."

"We've tried to bring him up right."

"You've done a good job."

"Is there anything I can do to help you with the team?"

I looked down at the tiny woman and smiled. "We only have a few substitutes," I said. "Can you shoot as well as your son?"

She delivered a high, loud laugh that filled the gym.

The next day during the shootaround before practice started, I stood at the center court jump circle watching Michael and the Whiz Kids closely. Edward R. Murrow stood beside me.

"Coach," he said, "why do you like little people so much?"

"I like all heights, all weights, all ages. I don't have any preferences. Whatever size people come in, that's what I like."

"But you have a soft spot for little people. Am I right?"

"You think so?"

"Yes."

"Well, I wasn't aware of it."

"It's obvious. Why do you think that is?"

"I have no idea."

"Was your father small?"

"No. He was a big, strapping catcher for the University of Minnesota. They called him Big Christy."

"Was your mother small?"

"What is this? The third degree?"

"I'm just wondering if your mother was small."

"Actually, she was quite tall."

"Well, maybe it was something you read, then. I like to think that we are what we read. I know you like *Gulliver's Travels*, with all the little Lilliputs scooting around."

"*Gulliver's Travels* isn't the only story I like."

"What else?"

I had been watching each of the players as they warmed up. Now I turned to give my full attention to Edward. "Even before I read *Gulliver's Travels*, when I was just a kid, my favorite book was *Down the River with the Teenie Weenies.*"

"Down the River with the *who?*"

"The Teenie Weenies."

"Coach, did your mother know you read smut?"

I laughed. "The book was not smut."

"It *sounds* like it was."

"The Teenie Weenies were characters who were so small they had their houses under a rosebush. They lived in the real world, except they were smaller and happier."

"Just like us."

"Well, yes. In a way. They were just little folks, hardly bigger than a thimble. You could have carried one of them in your pocket. One time one of them fell into an inkwell and they had to fish him out with a toothpick. They were professors, Africans, Jews, Japanese."

"They *were* just like us."

"Yes, I suppose they were. They were soldiers and sailors. They went to war against tiny bumblebees. Their army of toy soldiers fed on raisins and beans."

It was 2:15, time to start practice. I put my Acme Thunderer in the corner of my mouth but continued talking, so that the whistle whispered as I spoke. "I read *Down the River with the Teenie Weenies* over and over when I was a kid. It was almost the first thing I learned to read. In the story the Teenie Weenies discover an abandoned tiny boat and fix it up and sail down the river among the lily pads, dodging cattails."

"So, that's why you like little people so much?"

I took the whistle back out of my mouth. "That book taught me that it's the little people in the world who have the most fun. Little people are supposed to have short fuses or have been twisted in some other way by the curse of shortness. The myth is that they have to fight to prove themselves in a tall world."

"Coach, I've never had a fight in my life. I'm chickenshit. I can run like the wind from a fight."

"Edward, that's why I like *you* so much."

"Why? Because I'm windy?"

On Thursday, October 10, the Falcons met the Hillsdale Knights. The Knights had won five games in a row and were the only other undefeated team in the league. The game was at Crestmoor and promised to be a barnburner, but only a handful of students and fans showed up to watch.

The Hillsdale coach was Billy Wilkin. He grew up in San Bruno before Crestmoor was built. He learned to play basketball at outdoor courts all over the town, and he developed what he called his "windblown shot." But as a five-foot-three-inch high school freshman, he was too small to play regularly and he became a student of the game as he watched from the bench.

Wilkin described his own high school coach as "always mad," but as a coach at Hillsdale Wilkin was mild-mannered and always smiling. He rarely came off the bench to his feet or paced in front of it shouting frantic directions to his players. Gentleman Bill, his coaching colleagues called him. The only technical foul he ever drew was after an opposing coach shouted insults at an official. When Wilkin got up to explain that he didn't deserve the technical because he wasn't the one who had shouted the insults, the referee snarled at him, "You want another T?"

At the start of the "C" season he told his players, "Don't complain to me that you've got nothing to do. If your best friend is a basketball, you can go out and shoot shoot shoot all day long."

It was a reflection of how he learned the game, but his players told him, "Coach, there aren't any open gyms."

"Gyms?" he said. "The best basketball players in the world

learned to play on hardtop or dirt. Don't talk to me about gyms not being open. If you love the game you'll find someplace to shoot. All you need is a basketball."

Billy Wilkin has his Knights play a zone defense that slows down and frustrates the Falcons. At the end of the first quarter the Knights lead. The Falcons gather around me and listen carefully as I tell them, "I joked about you being sluggish against San Mateo. Now, you really are sluggish. You're not running. I'm gonna fall asleep. I know, I know. You're looking at a damn good zone defense. But the only way you can beat it is to get down the floor quickly and get a shot before they get a chance to set up their defense. Let's go! Stay awake! Let's run!"

The second quarter the Falcons race up and down the floor, leaving fiery plumes behind them as if they were shooting stars. Michael weaves and twists and scores again and again. At halftime the Falcons lead by 10 points.

"All right. That's more like it," *I tell them.*

Their lead lengthens in the third and fourth quarters. The Falcons win by 22 points. The sports editors do not hang up when Edward R. Murrow calls in the score. "Falcons Hand Knights First League Loss," *the editors report the next day.*

Michael leads the rout with 24 points, his best performance of the season. He is still leading the league in scoring. Jack Armstrong is not far behind him. Michael is convinced that nobody can beat them. But he says nothing to anybody except himself.

To start the second round of play the Falcons beat the Capuchino Mustangs by the same lopsided score as the first game. Jack Armstrong and the Professor lead the scoring. That same day, Hillsdale blows a 20-point halftime lead against San Mateo and loses on a last-second shot from under the basket.

It means that the Falcons have a two-game lead over Hillsdale in the run for the championship. The Falcons are 7-0 and seem to be coasting. I feel that the reasons teams lose are fixed and clear. But victory is fuzzy, and keeping players inspired after victory is hard.

Before the game with Mills I stumble and stutter through a locker-room speech that I hope is inspirational. But the Falcons can't be any more inspired and they hardly listen. "Chill out, Coach," they tell me. "Nobody can beat us."

The remark strikes a fateful "gong" in my head. But the Falcons beat Mills handily. This time it is the Professor who leads the scoring with his trademark bank shot off the backboard from either side of the basket. It is one of the most difficult shots in basketball, requiring the shooter to quickly calculate the exact angle of backboard deflection, depending on where he is on the floor. The Professor makes all seven of his bank shots. Salt scores five straight field goals. Fully recovered from his ankle injury, Suitcase rebounds with his usual Latvian tenacity.

The Falcons have won nine straight and the newspapers report, "Crestmoor Eyes Cage Title." Only the Hillsdale Knights, with two losses, have a chance to catch the Falcons. "We can win it all if we win two of our next three games," I tell the newspapers.

Crestmoor faces Burlingame again, this time in the Falcons' gym. I remind Michael and the Whiz Kids that they took the Panthers for granted last time and almost lost. Now I tell them, "History repeats itself. Do you know who said that?"

Jack Armstrong has an immediate answer. "George Bernard Shaw."

I nod. "So stay awake."

They take the floor and on the bench Edward R. Murrow turns to me. "There's only one thing I'm worried about," he says.

I am already worrying about a hundred dire eventualities, not the least of which is the team's conviction that they can't be beat. I wonder if I have overlooked worrying about something else. I look at Edward. "What are you worried about?"

He has his customary droll smile. "Coach," he asks, "could George Bernard Shaw shoot?"

The Falcons beat the Panthers by 40 points. It is their most lopsided victory of the year. Edward delivers a short speech in his radio voice in the jubilant locker room. "It will be a long time before another lightweight team is this good," he says.

Everybody whoops and pumps a fist, even Michael, who still leads the league in scoring and for once doesn't find something he did wrong during the game.

The Falcons enjoyed a bye and a day off. Again some of them took off for the Haight to unwind and gawk at the street freaks. There were now only two games remaining: San Mateo, then Hillsdale. In the locker room before the San Mateo game, Edward cupped one ear with his hand and told the whole world, "This could be the Falcons' toughest remaining opponent."

Only Michael took the warning seriously. He worried that the game would be trouble. Half of his worry was over what he knew was coming—more taunting. The other half was a vague foreboding that something *else* might be ahead waiting to ambush him.

His full name was Darnell Richard Ferguson, but his classmates shortened it to Fer, capturing his abbreviated size. He was born in 1950 in Natchez, Mississippi. He never learned who his father was and he was raised mostly by his grandparents. He went to a segregated Catholic elementary school.

Just across from the school an inviting city park was posted with "Whites Only" signs, contradicting the messages of tolerance and love that the nuns delivered daily to him and his black classmates.

His grandparents tried to explain the contradiction to him. "There are good people, and there are bad people," they said. "You just be good and do well in school. The bad people will be taken care of."

One day his grandfather got fed up with the racism and segregation at the tool company where he worked. He swore at his boss and shouted, "I quit!" Then he walked out.

That night the sheriff burst into their home and accused the grandfather of thievery. They searched his home for stolen tools. Outside a crowd gathered. For a black man to just walk off the job was unpardonable. Who did he think he was? It didn't matter that it had been over one hundred years since black people were bought and sold like sturdy mules. The grandfather was still no better than a slave chained to the labor of picking cotton or breaking hemp. "Kill him!" the crowd chanted. "Kill him!"

Not long after, seven members of the family packed themselves into one car and headed for what they hoped would be the open-mindedness of California, a state that tolerated freethinkers and social protestors. They got a home in Eastside in San Mateo. It wasn't that much better than Natchez. Darnell got a job delivering newspapers in a white neighborhood. But bicycling through the neighborhood, they looked at him with resentment, as if he had violated the same "whites only" restrictions that were posted in Natchez parks.

He enrolled at San Mateo High and as a one-hundred-pound freshman he distinguished himself as a promising wrestler. But in the years that followed at the annual athletic awards banquets, when the white athletes proudly stood to introduce their mothers and fathers, he felt isolation and estrangement worse than in Natchez.

His first heroes were Martin Luther King Jr. and Mahatma Gandhi. But during the Freedom Summer of 1964, the Civil Rights activists Michael Swerner, James Chaney, and Andrew Goodman were murdered in Mississippi and buried in an earthen dam. Then, with the murder of Martin Luther King, the self-defense messages of an angry Huey Newton began to make sense. Bad people weren't just providentially "taken care of" by a just world, as his grandparents had preached. They had to be opposed. They had to be fought against.

Because of the influences of his grandparents he could never be as intimidating to a white world as Tommy Smith and John Carlos, who had put their black-gloved fists in the air when they received their medals at the 1968 Olympics in Mexico City. But Darnell Ferguson was no less an advocate of black pride and power than they were.

After he first saw Michael Thompson on a basketball court, he marveled at Michael's talent. But why didn't he want to live in Eastside, Darnell asked himself, where there was at least warmth and all-day pickup basketball games among friends? Why did he want to live in all-white San Bruno, where just to survive he had to be an Uncle Tom who wore a space suit of tap dancing and smiles to protect himself from the cold inhospitality? It was, Darnell felt, like living on the surface of the moon. Meanwhile, he thought that whatever acceptance there might have been in San Bruno for Michael was only a form of white tap dancing to cover up their guilt for over one hundred years of racism.

When he got off the bus for the game at Crestmoor, Darnell wasn't alone in his convictions. After the first humiliating defeat at the hands of Crestmoor his San Mateo teammates had decided they couldn't beat the Falcons unless they could neutralize Michael Thompson. They knew that the taunting had gotten to him in The Pit. To win at Crestmoor they would have to get on his nerves again with taunting.

It started even before either team had changed into their uniforms. "That's him!" somebody shouted and pointed to Michael as both teams entered the locker room. "That's him." It was as if they were identifying the enemy.

When the Bearcats step onto the floor of the Crestmoor gym there is one more incentive for them. There are less than one hundred fans in the quiet gym, and as the Bearcats warm up, a few of those fans hurl racial epithets at San Mateo's black players. They are "monkeys," "coons," "shines." Then, just as soon as the game starts, somebody throws a tobacco pipe at Darnell Ferguson. It hits him in the face, clatters on the floor like a spilled marble, then is kicked aside by a player.

In the first few minutes the Falcons jump off to a slim lead. In the struggle for rebounds and the effort to fight through screens, players stagger and fall. After a defensive rebound Michael tries to dribble the full length of the floor but is knocked off his feet at midcourt. He pops to his feet and as the Bearcat players loom over him, he has to use an arm bar to push them away.

All the Bearcats are angry over the catcalls and epithets, but it is Darnell Ferguson who plays with the most intensity. He fights his way through Salt and Suitcase to grab a rebound on his own missed shot. He thrashes his arms and tries to put the ball back up. Again he misses, and again he seizes the rebound and goes back up. This time both Salt and Suitcase are hanging on his arms. He scores and is fouled. At the free-throw line before he shoots, he angrily hammer-dribbles the ball three times before he makes the free throw.

Before the first quarter is over a Bearcat crashes the Falcons' backboard on a missed shot and holds the ball tightly to his belly to protect it. With Falcons still around him he twists his shoulders so that his distended elbows fly like sharp rotor blades.

Salt suddenly cups his nose with both hands and falls to his knees. The officials stop play for an injury time out.

I rush onto the floor. Salt gets back on his feet. "What's the matter?" I ask him.

"I'm okay." He is still cupping his nose.

"What's the matter with your nose?"

". . . elbow," is all he says, meaning one of those rotor elbows has cracked him in the nose.

I part Salt's hands to inspect the nose, which is red and crooked. I turn and shout to the bench, "Esposto!"

"—I'm okay," Salt insists. "I'm okay!"

"Esposto!" I repeat.

A Crestmoor coach who is watching the game takes Salt into the coaches' office and begins pasting strips of white tape over his nose. What has happened in less than five minutes of the game is brutal action that I feel will lead to more than broken noses. Michael is getting the worst of it, although as they stand in a circle and I give instructions to Esposto on who he is guarding, Michael's head is up for once and he is clearly angry.

"Michael," I say, "are you all right?"

He nods.

"You sure?"

He nods again.

Time in.

ELEVEN

Uncle Tom

"Rabbit ears" was what they called referees who were said to be vulnerable to even whispers of criticism from a coach or his bench. I had never gotten a technical foul for my bench behavior. I made it a point never even to speak to officials during a game, especially those with "rabbit ears." I felt that in most cases harping about the officiating only backfired and brought resentment that officials took out on the complaining coach's team.

But as I left the floor I confronted one of the officials. "Get control of this game!" I barked.

The referee glared at me. "I thought you liked a wide-open, loose game. I thought you wanted to let the boys run."

"You're letting it get out of control."

The official was still glaring at me. "A few bumps here and there—those are just good no-calls."

Michael races down the floor with the ball. A defender clips him in the hips and he spins and loses the ball.

A whistle blows, finally.

When Michael steps to the free-throw line to shoot the foul, the taunting that he knows is coming begins.

"You don't belong up here with all these honkies."

"You belong down with us."

"We're gonna beat you and your white boys."

"Hey," they whisper out of earshot of the officials, "Uncle Tom."

"This is exactly what I expected," Michael tells himself. The quarter ends with the Falcons leading, 14–10.

Salt returns from the locker room to the bench. His nose is smothered in white tape. The subs on the bench grimace at the sight of his face. It is not even clear that he still has a nose somewhere under all that white tape.

"I'm okay," he says. "I'm okay."

He goes back in the game for Esposto. And as the action flies up and down the floor, the taunts are no longer whispered but called out. Then on a rebound Michael is pushed from behind so hard that he lurches into other Bearcat players, who knock him away like a pinball.

Michael freezes on the floor and stares angrily at the San Mateo players. Edward R. Murrow leaps to his feet on the bench and turns to me. "This is vicious. What the hell are you gonna do?"

I take a time-out. With the entire team gathered around me, I look only at Michael.

"They are working on you," I tell him.

Michael has his head up and there is defiance in his face.

"They are working on you," I repeat.

Michael nods.

"We can hear what they're calling you."

The entire bench and the players on the floor have heard the taunts.

"They can say all they want," Michael says. "But if they hit me—"

He leaves the eventuality of getting hit hanging.

"Michael, they're going to get mad as hell and they will take a swing at you. "

"I'll keep my cool," he says.

"Good. Good. Whoever takes a swing at you, I want you to drop to the floor and cover up. Don't swing back. If you do, you'll both get thrown out."

I am calling for restraint that the entire team knows is unlikely. Who in the world isn't going to swing back if they get sucker punched? But everybody nods. Everybody agrees. Michael can't do anything to get himself thrown out of the game.

"And I don't want anybody else swinging back," I say. "If there are fisticuffs stay out of the way. Back off. Back off. If anybody gets thrown out, we're in trouble."

Time in.

San Mateo scores. The Falcons counterattack and fly down the floor. It is only a matter of seconds before a shot goes up. The ball bounces high and then hangs on the rim for a second before it drops off. The delay gives Michael time to get to the boards and leap high to curl in the rebound. He lands with his back turned to the San Mateo players who are trying to reach around him to steal the ball.

Michael struggles to free himself of a bear hug from behind him. He begins to fall and is almost doing the splits before he recovers his balance. Then he is knocked on the head from behind. Michael drops the ball and wheels around to face Darnell Ferguson.

The two glare at each other. Their looks say, "C'mon. C'mon. Throw a punch at me. I dare you."

For Ferguson the catcalls and the insults and the pipe thrown at him from the bleachers—it is all Natchez again. A "Whites Only" sign may not be posted on the Crestmoor gym doors, but the spirit is there.

He swings and lands a punch in Michael's face. Michael staggers and steadies himself. In the brief second before he reacts, he glances at me on the bench. "Coach," his glance says, "I gotta do what I gotta do."

Michael swings and catches Ferguson in the mouth. It is Ferguson now who totters briefly and has to steady himself before he and Michael are both swinging.

It has erupted so fast that no whistles have blown yet. The players on the floor are only observing in shock. What in the hell is happening?

Two, three, four, then all five San Mateo players and several off the bench who have rushed onto the floor are now in the fight. They push Michael up against the blue wall mat and swing at him. He is trapped and swings back wildly, landing few punches but at least keeping the Bearcats at bay.

The Falcon players on the floor are backing away. I struggle at our bench to push back the substitutes. "Sit down!" I shout, "sit down!"

But Michael is getting the worst of it and still swinging wildly. Suddenly, he sees only a blue flash out of the corner of his good eye. It is one of his friends whom Doris Thompson has identified as a troublemaker. In an instant he is beside Michael and the two of them are up against the blue mat, swinging furiously. An official finally blows his whistle but nobody stops swinging. Another of Michael's friends comes out of the bleachers and joins the melee. Then others. It becomes a free-for-all with players and a few fans and Michael's friends swinging and kicking or trying to wrestle somebody to the floor.

A gym that has been as hushed as a funeral parlor is filled with jeering and hooting. Both officials are blowing their whistles to stop the slugfest. Somebody at the scorer's bench is pushing the button repeatedly for the buzzer. It blares in the gym like a klaxon horn warning, "Air raid! Air Raid! Air Raid!" More fans come out of the stands and try to rip fighters away from the melee. But those who try to intercede are quickly sucked into the fight.

I turn to my bench. "Don't any of you move!" I shout.

Then I run to the edge of the struggling bodies and begin bear-hugging and ripping at the tiny combatants. I join the two officials whose whistles are shrieking. We are all Gullivers in the thick of struggling Lilliputs, but we are powerless to stop it.

It is two more minutes of swinging, pushing, jabbing, and kicking before the knot of fighters dissolves from sheer exhaustion.

The officials eject both Ferguson and Michael. One official escorts Ferguson to his bench, where he discovers that he has a chipped tooth. The other official stands face to face with Michael and hollers, "You're out of here!"

He points to the door, meaning that Michael has to leave the gym.

"Why does he go?" I snarl at the official. "He didn't throw the first punch."

It is a token protest. I know that it doesn't matter who threw the first punch. Both fighters go. I have already warned Michael and the rest of the team of just that eventuality.

I leave the floor. I detour past the Bearcats bench and bark at Coach Snider for not taking Darnell Ferguson out of the game before the fight, to let him cool down.

Once back at my own bench it takes me only a moment to pick a substitute for Michael. In the event the game continues to be a wrestling match I want my toughest, most aggressive player in the game. That is tiny Darrell Hirashima.

"Darrell," I call. "You're in." I glance at the scorer's table to see who is replacing Ferguson. Then I turn back to Darrell. "You've got number twelve. I don't know what he can do. But it doesn't matter. You're covering every Bearcat on the floor."

The circle of Falcons whoops and Darrell claws the thick shock of black hair from his forehead. With his baby face and just five feet tall, he hardly has a fierce look about him.

But he will push and shove and poke at his man as if he is preparing to lock his arms around him and throw him to the floor and pin him. If Bearcat fists fly again the takedown by Darrell will be immediate.

"We've got work to do," I tell the Falcons before play resumes. "We're here to play basketball." Then I look at Jack Armstrong and the Professor. "You two have to step it up. Keep running!"

Time in.

Through the rest of the quarter the Bearcats play with a fury that was missing entirely when they met in The Pit, where they had been embarrassed by the Falcons. Now their pride is at stake, along with the Bearcat reputation as the reigning kings of lightweight basketball on the Peninsula.

At halftime the score is tied. In the team room Michael has already showered and changed back into his street clothes and his fedora. I stand with my back to a blackboard and talk, but nobody is listening. They are all reliving the nightmares of the fight.

In the third quarter the Falcons are unusually tentative, as if they don't want to do anything aggressive that would lead to another altercation. They miss easy layups and rebounds skitter just out of their reach. Only Darrell Hirashima, who is all over the floor, is playing with his usual fierce defensive intensity.

At the end of the third quarter the Falcons are behind by 3 points. I point to the Bearcat huddle. "That is the same team we beat by 30 points in The Pit. They are still wearing the same jerseys and the same shoes. They haven't grown. And this isn't The Pit, with unforgiving rims and bad lighting. This is our gym. This is where we run everybody right out the gym door."

The teams trade baskets again in the fourth quarter. Realizing that they are in the fight of their lives, Jack

Armstrong and the Professor and Suitcase take over on the Falcons' offense. But with less than a minute to go, the Falcons trail by 5 points.

I take a time-out and point to the clock. Only fifty seconds remaining. "Plenty of time," I say hollowly.

As soon as play is resumed, a loose ball skitters from one player to another until the Bearcats recover it and score, widening their lead to 7 points.

The Falcons counterattack and the Professor scores immediately on a twenty-foot jump shot: the Falcons again trail by 5.

The Bearcats miss and I take our last time-out to set up the Falcons' Solar Eclipse play, a double screen that gives Jack Armstrong the ball along the baseline. He moves to his right to get to the basket and is blocked. He spins and curls away from the baseline and is almost at the free-throw line before he stops and jumps. He hangs in the air for a half second longer than usual, to draw a careful bead on the basket. I think he has taken himself out of the ordinary rhythm of his shot and will miss.

The shot is good! Twenty seconds left. The Bearcats' lead is down to 3 points.

As soon as they inbound the ball, the Bearcats get the ball quickly to half court and take a time-out. Coach Snider drops to the floor while his players stand in a tight circle so that he can draw a chalk diagram of what he wants them to do.

At our bench I tell the Falcons, "Be as tough as you've ever been on defense when they inbound the ball. But don't foul. Don't foul. If you pick off the inbound pass take an immediate time-out. They'll probably set up to get Bobo Groves the ball. He's their best ball handler. If they can get the ball to him, he'll just dribble to run out the clock."

I put my hand on Darrell Hirashima's shoulder. "Darrell, you got Bobo. I want you to play him so tight he'll think *you're his own jersey. If you steal the ball off his dribble, take a time-out."*

Before the time-out is over, I shout to the official standing near our huddle. I tell him that if we manage to pick off a pass or steal the ball, we'll take an immediate time-out. "Be ready for it," I tell him.

He gives me an odd look, as if I'm a desperate dreamer hoping to do the impossible in just fifteen seconds.

Time in. I squint at the scribble of chalk lines on the floor in front of the Bearcats' bench. Several of the Bearcat players quickly use their shoes to scrub the chalk diagram off the floor.

The official hands the ball to one of the Bearcats and chops one hand to tick off the five-second time limit for inbounding the ball. His count is at four when the Bearcats finally get the ball inbounds to Bobo Groves.

The rest of the Bearcats move down to the baseline and leave Bobo all alone just across midcourt. He dribbles left, right, left again. Darrell Hirashima is in a deep crouch, like a wrestler on a mat with an opponent, slapping and clawing and swiping at Bobo in an effort to get a good grip for a takedown. But each time Darrell jumps at Bobo for the takedown, Bobo slips sideways or backward and escapes. There are fans crowded onto the floor at the end of the gym. They have been standing and shouting themselves hoarse since halftime, when reports of the game brawl flashed around the school and drew them to the gym, hoping to see another brawl.

"Get him!" they shout to Darrell. "Get him!"

I am certain that he will do just that, because we have narrowed the Bearcats' lead to 3 points. San Mateo is panicked, desperately trying to hold on by relying on their best player to run out the clock and take them to victory.

But momentum is with us. Momentum. It is the most

meaningless cliché in athletic competition, I think, worse than "winning one for the Gipper." But in this gym in these last few seconds, it takes on a sudden meaning for me.

Momentum! Momentum! Momentum! It echoes in my head as clear as a gunshot.

I am certain now that Darrell Hirashima is going to steal the ball off Bobo on his dribble. We'll take an immediate time-out. In the few second left, we'll run our Solar Eclipse play again. Jack Armstrong won't miss.

But the uncertain half of me says, "What if he misses?"

"He won't miss," I argue with myself.

"But what if he does?" a small voice inside me says.

I am too much in the grip of my fantasy to listen to my own small voice. I am certain that Jack Armstrong will float inside for the shot. The shot will sink into the net as a whistle blows and the horn sounds. Foul! With no time on the clock, and those hoarse fans croaking and screaming, Jack Armstrong will step to the free-throw line and coolly sink the free throw.

Tie game!

Overtime!

But before my fantasy can be realized, the buzzer sounds with Bobo Groves still dribbling. The Falcons lose by 3 points.

Crestmoor fans, particularly Michael's friends who had entered the floor fight, were furious. The effort to get under Michael's black skin was an outrage. Immediately after the defeat those rankled fans rushed onto the floor to confront the Bearcat players.

Crestmoor faculty and coaches had to form two lines to hold back angry fans when the Bearcats left the gym and headed for their bus. For the Bearcat players it was like running a gauntlet.

Michael had spent the rest of the game in the locker room.

He had no idea how the game had ended. When his teammates entered the locker room, he wondered, "What happened?"

The answer came in a sad chorus: "We lost."

I gathered the defeated and dejected Falcons in their team room. "I don't like what happened any more than you do," I said. "The officials are as much to blame as anybody."

"We should protest!" Edward R. Murrow said.

They all agreed. Nobody said *why* they should protest. A bad call? Scoring error? Some technical violation of the rules, like an illegal player or a jersey number that wasn't permitted by the rules?

"Coach, are you gonna file a protest?"

"No. You can't protest bad behavior."

They accepted it grudgingly. Then they waited for whatever else I intended to say. Was I going to chastise them all for not joining the fight? Most of them were hanging their heads and felt bad enough already. Besides, how could I blame them? I was the one who had admonished them to "back away, back away" if punches were thrown.

Or maybe I would criticize Michael for not dropping to the floor and covering up. But I remembered poor Shylock in *The Merchant of Venice*, who tells his tormentors that he is no different than they are. If he is stabbed, he bleeds. If he is wronged, he wants revenge.

Michael was stabbed. Michael was wronged. He wanted revenge.

"I don't want any of you to draw the wrong conclusions from what happened," I finally said. "It would be easy to blame the Bearcats for swinging first. But that's not *why* it happened. You read the papers. You know what's going on all over the country." I looked at Edward R. Murrow, who had helped organize the lunchtime panel presentation after Dr. King was assassinated. "It's happening right here."

There was much more that I wanted to say. Michael wasn't

an Uncle Tom, I wanted to explain. Uncle Toms *pretended* to be the happy-go-lucky, subservient people their white oppressors imagined them to be. Michael Thompson was exactly the opposite. He wasn't pretending to be anybody other than who he was, a shy, tiny, half-blind black pilgrim in a white world.

But what could I say that wouldn't sound pedantic? What could I say that wouldn't sound like I was in my classroom lecturing about poor Shylock while my audience sat in their uniforms dripping sweat and hanging their heads? Only Michael had his head up, his chin pointed with defiance and anger.

"No practice tomorrow," I told them. "Next practice is Monday. Go home. Forget about the loss."

It wasn't so much the loss that still angered Michael. He knew the Falcons were the better team. He knew he wasn't an Uncle Tom. But after hearing that the Falcons had lost he was even madder about what had happened to him during the game.

After I told them all to go home, Michael left the locker room in a hurry and ran for the Bearcats' bus.

"Come on outside," he shouted at the bus windows.

Nobody on the bus moved.

He leaped the steps inside the bus and lunged down the aisle to confront the Bearcats who had gang-jumped him. It took one of the San Mateo coaches, who was twice Michael's size, to bar his way, then pick him up and lift him off the bus.

When he got home his mother already knew about the fight. "Michael Ralph, what happened?" She was wearing her stern, willow-switch face.

"Some guy was buggin' me and buggin' me."

His mother waited for him to explain more.

"Then he hit me."

Her face was set with suspicion. "Did you hit him first?"

"No."

She nodded. Michael was her precious, tiny son, whom she had taught to do no wrong. "Well, did you hit him back good?"

"Yes."

After the San Mateo defeat I spent the weekend trying to figure out how to treat the fight incident. I decided to discuss it with Michael and the Whiz Kids at a brief team meeting on Monday. At the meeting I would help them sort through all the reasons why it had happened. I knew it would be a strained and clumsy discussion, because I hardly understood the reasons myself, but to ignore the incident completely seemed unwise.

Meanwhile Michael remained angry over the weekend after the San Mateo game. He had seen the disaster coming but he had been powerless to stop it. It wasn't just that he hadn't been able to stop the Bearcats. He hadn't been able to stop himself. It suggested a world of fate and inevitability that he had spent most of his life defying.

After Michael's sight had been restored in Oklahoma, one of the first things he had seen was a movie-screen world of black and white. As much as he wanted to put that divided world out of his mind, that weekend he couldn't. There were too many reminders. The headline news on Sunday was that a black activist teacher at a nearby college was suspended because of the provocative material in his course on race relations. At the same college a "striking sophomore beauty" who served as the college's black queen removed the sparkling tiara as soon as she was crowned and raised a fist to symbolize black power.

That weekend Michael also worried that his teammates

would focus only on the black-on-black circumstances of the incident. From it they would draw the conclusion that all blacks were hotheaded. But there was nothing about it that was hotheaded. The Bearcats' taunting had been a tactic as carefully designed as their Heart Attack play. That it had worked and gotten Michael thrown out of the game made matters even worse.

On Monday morning, November 4, a letter came to the school from the Bearcats' captain and now the league's leading scorer, Bobo Groves. Addressed to the Crestmoor "C" team and coach, the letter said Groves and his teammates wanted to express their sorrow over the fight. "We hope you will accept our apologies," Groves wrote. But remarks from "certain spectators" in the stands who had called the Bearcats "coons" and "monkeys" were not justified and could not be accepted.

Monday afternoon I watched Michael and the Whiz Kids shoot around before practice. It was then that I changed my mind about a team meeting. I watched them dribble and turn and jump and shoot and then playfully chase after their shots. For all of them basketball was clearly an antidote, a relief from the tedium of school and the predictability of San Bruno. It was also relief from the burden of trying to understand what had happened in the fight, and why. Discussing it, beyond the brief effort I had already made in the locker room after the game, with all of them hanging their heads, would only serve to root it in their memories like a sliver that only lodges itself deeper during clumsy efforts to remove it.

What was foremost in everybody's mind that Monday at practice was the last game of the season, scheduled for Thursday of that week against the Hillsdale Knights, who were now 9-2 and one game behind the Falcons, at 10-1. For Michael, his goal of going undefeated had been lost. The one remaining goal was not to be cochampions with Hillsdale but champions outright. Victory against the Knights would assure that. It would prove that the loss to the Bearcats had been a fluke. It would prove that the Falcons were as good as everyone said they were.

TWELVE

Nerb

Tuesday morning I got a call from Billy Wilkin.

"I hear rumors about a fight," the Hillsdale coach said.

"Michael Thompson and a few of the black kids from San Mateo tangled in the second quarter. It was an explosion that was over quickly."

It hadn't been over quickly and it was more an *implosion* than an explosion, I felt. For the San Mateo black players, all their energy and anger had been directed inward toward Michael rather than outward toward the real sources of their troubles.

"Well, that's not why I called," Wilkin said.

I waited for him to explain.

"We're scheduled to play Thursday afternoon in our gym, right?"

"Right."

"Why don't we play the game Friday *night?*" Wilkin proposed. "It's for the championship."

Hillsdale's gym was huge, with a long court and high banks of pull-out bleachers. A Thursday afternoon game with only a scatter of fans in those expansive bleachers would make it appear as if it were a game of no consequence. But a Friday night game would draw a crowd. There were no football games. The features at the local theaters looked dull. The television programming looked even duller. Moving the lightweight game to Friday night would give working parents a chance to see their sons play. Crestmoor students, hungry to see a championship in anything, would help pack the gym.

"Billy," I said, "that's the best idea you've ever had."

"I'll talk to my principal," Wilkin offered.

"I'm sure mine won't object," I said.

On Tuesday it was confirmed. The two teams would meet Friday night at seven o'clock at Hillsdale, a school that stood more as an identical twin to Crestmoor than an unrelated, hostile opponent. Hillsdale had opened in 1955 and had been the first of four new schools added in less than a decade to the San Mateo Union High School District. It had been constructed as the first case in the district of the architectural Brutalism that eventually defined Crestmoor, with an "inherent flexibility of design."

If flexibility was intended to be Hillsdale's mantra, it was reflected mainly in the modular architecture. Otherwise, Hillsdale students complained in those early years that there was too much *in*flexibility, "too much conformity," especially in the rules of Ivy League dress. Girls rebelled against that conformity with short, tight skirts. If they wanted to wear tailored slacks or pantsuits they had to apply for the privilege on a three-by-five card. Meanwhile, boys sported long hair and a forbidden "beat look." The school suspended two students who encouraged classmates to attend a Peace and Freedom Party rally where Mario Savio, leader of the Free Speech Movement, spoke about the rigidity of American culture. A "student court" was formed to combat the problem of campus litter. After the litter didn't go away a student "litter patrol" roamed the campus during lunch and issued citations. When the school talked about its diversity it proudly pointed to a foreign-exchange student from Germany.

Conformity in dress, a spotless, litter-free campus, a student body short on diversity—it was precisely what defined Crestmoor. And like Crestmoor, the Hillsdale student body was a mix of working-class families from a flatland of post–World War II bungalows and "junior executive" families from spacious hillside homes.

By 1968 the two schools stood as look-alike bookends for the district. Neither was a crosstown rival of the other. Both could boast, as the entire district did, of having some of the best teachers and the most innovative teaching programs in the nation. Had it not been for what was at stake—a championship title that had been two months in the making—that Friday night game might have promised to be no more than a contest between friendly twins.

There was one more reason why a championship game between two teams of basketball bantams caught the eye of the Peninsula. His name was "Wee Willie" Slocum, and in the elections that had been held on Tuesday of that week, Slocum had entered the race for the California State Assembly.

A year earlier Slocum had run for Congress against Shirley Temple Black and Paul McCloskey, a Republican who strongly opposed the Vietnam War. But it was Wee Willie Slocum who had captured the hearts, if not the votes, of Peninsula citizens. At just four feet ten inches and 103 pounds, he was an ex-jockey who smoked a briar pipe, wore a straw hat frayed at the brim, and had shaggy hair. "It would be unfair," he joked, "to blame the muddled state of my mind on appearance only."

He was anything but muddled in campaign speeches in which he also objected to the Vietnam War. To end the war, he promised that he would talk to tiny Ho Chi Minh and "meet him on his level." He wanted women in combat because the war should be made to hurt for all people. "Young men shouldn't be made to die for us in Vietnam," he said, "because we think they owe us that much for the privilege of having been born here."

Now, in his write-in campaign for a seat in the California State Assembly, he complained that traditional politics ignored the little guy. "As a little guy," he promised, "I will look after the little guy." He was running, he said, for little guys all across the country. "I know the tragedy of having a car repossessed." When he lost the assembly election Slocum told his supporters, "I am little enough to cry."

It was a message of self-effacing honesty and Will Rogers plain talk that made sense to even big folks, and the political news he made that week before the Crestmoor-Hillsdale game endeared him to voters on the Peninsula. Being small was no liability. Being small shouldn't mean being ignored. Being small meant excitement and a fresh perspective on life. It was the perfect preparation for a basketball game between two teams of undersized high school boys.

It had been cold and rainy off and on all that week. By noon on Friday it was still overcast during a pep rally at lunch in the Crestmoor Great Court. The pep band played in the right key. Yell leaders jumped and cheered. It seemed appropriate fanfare for a thrilling game.

Friday afternoon the temperature warmed and the skies cleared, as if to suggest that the entire cosmos was grooming itself for the game. Michael and the Whiz Kids were unusually quiet on their bus ride down the Peninsula later that afternoon. When they entered the Hillsdale gym and filed into the visitors' locker room, only one side of the bleachers had been pulled out and it held just a sprinkle of fans. It was, I thought, exactly the opposite of what Billy Wilkin and I had expected. It would be another ignored lightweight game, with few fans and no media attention.

In the Hillsdale locker room, Billy Wilkin reminds the Knights that much has happened since that first, lopsided loss to Crestmoor. Coming into the second round they have won five games in a row and nobody can beat them. "We've improved so much since that loss to Crestmoor," he tells his players. "I don't know how many of you believe me. But I want you to believe in yourselves." He pauses to let them summon up that belief. "San Mateo just beat Crestmoor. We beat San Mateo." He pauses again. "We're right in this game tonight."

In the Crestmoor locker room, I speak quietly about what they have fought their way through. Michael had wrung himself out like a wet towel to make weight. Despite the mayhem of that last minute of play at Burlingame, the entire team had somehow held on to win. When I worried about a short bench, Jack Armstrong and the Professor and Salt had recruited Darrell Hirashima. Suitcase's ankle injury had crippled him to a limp. Relying on the same grit that had enabled his mother to walk three hundred miles to freedom during World War II, he had returned to the lineup quickly. Salt had played through a broken nose. "I'm okay," he had kept repeating. "I'm okay." The only time they had stumbled was against San Mateo. Now came the true test. Could they get back to being the high-flying Whiz Kids who shot every ten seconds and left trails of blue stardust as they flew down the floor?

Michael hardly hears my words. He is too worried about the fact that both his mother and father will be in the stands for the first time. Would his mother hold him up to the same demanding measure of performance on a basketball court as she did in life? Would his mother and father even appreciate how important the game was to him? They had pushed him into a white world, and in the process he had elevated himself, not just because they had pushed him but because he had willed it.

The rest of the team is even more nervous than Michael. They may have all succeeded in putting the fight in the back of their minds, but the disappointment of the loss to San Mateo is still keen. How had they lost? How had they let it happen? Losing again, this time to the Knights, a team they had beaten easily in the first round, would be an even greater disappointment.

I stand at the team room blackboard and go over what to expect from Hillsdale. "They will try to run," I say. "We know that. They may not run as much or as fast as you, but they'll run. That means you backpedal, backpedal. They've won five in a row. They'll be higher than kites. But they'll also be tight. Because a lot more is at stake for them than us. If they don't win, they've got nothing. Zero. Zilch. For us, win or lose, we have a share of the championship."

A share of the championship? The minute I say it I know it is wrong. Nobody, certainly not me, wants a "share" of the championship. They want it free and clear, the whole shebang, lock, stock, and barrel. Children "share" toys in nursery school. Nobody, least of all Michael and the Whiz Kids, wants to share a championship.

"Okay," I say. "Listen up." It is my habitual strategy for moving off sticking points or my own misspeak. "Hillsdale's best player by far is Dan Nerby." I pause to look at Michael. Jack Armstrong is as good, perhaps even a better defender. But now I want to demonstrate to Michael that nobody has lost confidence in him because of the fight.

"Michael," I say, "you've got Nerby. He's good. But if he scores one damn point, I'll wind up panhandling for grass in the Haight."

It is Edward R. Murrow who appreciates my joke the most. "Coach," he says, "you don't have to go to the Haight. I can get you a baggie of African Yohimbe bark right in San Bruno."

Nobody laughs. Especially not Michael, who is already focusing on how he will stop Dan Nerby.

At the end of his long career coaching basketball, Billy Wilkin remembered that Dan Nerby was the most competitive athlete he had ever coached. He was small but he played like a powerful lion trying to break out of the five-foot-seven-inch cage of his own body. He could play defense, rebound, pass, and most of all shoot.

It was his brother Tim, five years older and born with cerebral palsy, who had helped mold his little brother into a superb athlete. Doctors told the Nerbys that their son Tim would never walk or talk, but after fifteen years of therapy and a foot brace worn throughout his childhood, he grew to be six feet three inches and nearly a foot taller than his little brother. Despite his limitations, Tim became a formidable opponent in one-on-one basketball games, which were always standoffs. Tim could not stop his speedy little brother if he drove to the basket. Dan could not stop Tim when he backed and pushed his way into the key, then turned and shot.

The two brothers became inseparable. They shared the same bedroom. At night they could see when the lights came on at the basketball court at a nearby park. If players were choosing sides when the Nerby brothers arrived and nobody wanted Tim Nerby on their side, it was Dan, whose talent they all wanted, who told them, "If my brother can't play, I'm not playing."

They played full court, rain or shine, sometimes until two or three in the morning. Tim's left hand was useless. But with his huge right hand he would tap rebounds to teammates to start a fast break. If they had to set up he learned to plant himself in the key and palm the ball off the dribble and deliver a sweeping shot.

"There isn't an obstacle I can't overcome," Tim Nerby told his little brother.

It was an object lesson that made Dan Nerby determined to overcome the limitations of his size and to fight through exhaustion or pain in basketball. During games he broke fingers, sprained ankles, was slashed and cut and pounded and bloodied. In the fight for rebounds against taller players he took elbow shots to the head that floored him. But he quickly popped to his feet and resumed his aggressive play. He fouled out of almost every game he played. His coaches complained that he was no good to them on the bench and they told him to tone down his game. But he was too fiercely competitive to change his style of play. In the team picture taken before the season started, Dan Nerby sat alone in the front row bearing a scowl and a set jaw that reflected how unrelenting he was in basketball. Meanwhile, Hillsdale's fans loved him. "Nerb! Nerb! Nerb!" they chanted if he sat on the bench. "Nerb! Nerb! Nerb!"

THIRTEEN

Rick

I told Michael what to expect from Nerby. "He'll be number fourteen. He's quick going either way. He's strong. So strong that Coach Wilkin will have him post up. If he can't muscle over you, he'll sneak a shot under you."

I pointed at Suitcase and Salt. "Nerby will scrap for every rebound, offense and defense. He's got quick hands. If you come down with a rebound he'll try to steal the ball from you." I turned back to Michael and Jack Armstrong. "If they press us, he'll be on the point. If you get careless with your dribble he'll pick you clean."

Somebody pounded on the team room door, indicating it was time for the Falcons to take the floor. I quickly reminded the others whom they would be guarding. None of them, I felt, deserved the attention of Nerby. "Michael will have his hands full with Nerby. All of you," I said and then repeated it, "—*all of you*, be ready to help Michael out with Nerby. Okay. Let's go," I finished.

They jogged onto the floor along a narrow corridor at the end of the bleachers. All year long they had worn all-white or all-blue uniforms. For the first time that season they were wearing blue jerseys and white pants. They also wore the varsity warm-up jackets that had betrayed my inability to spell Falcons. Still, the jackets and the blue-and-white uniforms made a flashy combination that I hoped would quicken their play, even if no fans showed up.

But as soon as they came onto the floor all of them were nearly stopped in their tracks. The far side bleachers had been pulled out to accommodate fans. Both sides of the bleachers were packed. Colorful butcher-paper signs had been pasted in place on the gym walls. On one wall, the signs read, "Wing the Falcons!" "Chicken Little Was a Falcon!" On the opposite side: "It's Nighty-Night for the Knights!" "Lance the Knights!" Room had been made at the scorer's table for several Peninsula sportswriters, among them Edward R. Murrow in his trademark denim sport coat and cravat. Behind the sportswriters a movie camera on a rigged platform at the top row was turned to record the Falcons' arrival in the gym. At each end of the court, spectators who couldn't find a seat were crowded two deep up against the gym walls. Both pep bands were playing at once. Yell leaders pumped their pom-poms and jumped and kicked. The Knights had already taken the floor and Hillsdale fans were still standing and cheering. Now, with the appearance of the Falcons, their fans came to their feet and shouted in an effort to drown out everything else.

Michael looked for his parents. But the deafening noise seemed to turn the packed bleachers into just a blur. "Maybe they didn't come," he said.

Jack Armstrong, who might have taken attention and approval for granted, could not believe the size of the crowd.

Suitcase glanced at both bleachers. "This isn't real," he thought. "This is a dreamland."

"I will never forget this," Salt knew. "I will never forget this."

The Professor shouted, "Wow!" The noise was deafening and the gym was filled with the same exhilaration that filled his house when his father hosted loud jam sessions for his jazz friends.

Among that sea of faces were almost all of the San Mateo Bearcats, among then Darnell Ferguson. They were there mainly to watch what promised to be a good game. Who won didn't matter to them. What had happened between them and Michael didn't matter either. They had beaten both Hillsdale and Crestmoor in the second round. They were convinced that they were better than both teams.

Both pep bands are playing when the officials toot their whistles to start the game. Nobody can hear their whistles and, like sheepdogs, the officials round up the players and bring them to the center jump circle. Suitcase controls the tip to Jack Armstrong, who immediately starts full speed for the basket. At the free-throw circle he pulls up for a jump shot, and misses.

Nerby rebounds and head up the floor quickly. He passes the Hillsdale bench. His parents and his brother Tim are seated immediately behind the Hillsdale substitutes. "You can do it!" Tim shouts.

It is encouragement meant to remind his little brother that nothing, not even a good opponent, is too difficult to overcome.

But as soon as Nerby enters the front court on his dribble, Michael smothers him. He tries to drive left. Michael is there. He tries to drive right. Michael is there again. Finally Nerby spins and manages to get to the free-throw line before other Falcons are collapsing on him. He jumps and a picket fence of arms is blocking his shot. He pulls back the ball to his waist and shovels a pass to an open teammate off to his left.

The teammate fakes the baseline, then drives toward the middle. When he reaches the free-throw line he jumps. It is a picture-perfect shot. His body hangs straight and loose. The ball is cradled gently in his right hand. He releases the shot softly and scores.

2–0. Hillsdale.

I jump to my feet. Who the hell is that? I wonder. I have no recollection of even seeing the player on the floor in the first game with Hillsdale.

Suitcase snatches the ball almost before it is out of the net and steps out of bounds. The Professor is already deep but covered. Suitcase throws his full-court bullet pass anyway. The pass is picked off and the Knights race back up the floor and score again.

4–0. Hillsdale.

Suitcase is already out of bounds with the ball, ready to throw full court again when I call for a time-out. But the Hillsdale fans are screaming so loud that nobody can hear me. The Professor is covered so Suitcase finds Jack Armstrong at half court, directly in front of the Falcons' bench, and I make a T with both hands and stick it in Jack Armstrong's face.

Time out. Falcons.

My instructions in the huddle are brief. "They want to run. Okay. Good. You can run faster than they can. Now go out there and pick up the pace."

Time in.

The Falcons push the ball up the floor and the Professor finds himself open on the baseline. It is his best range and his favorite spot on the floor. He doesn't miss.

4–2. Knights.

Again Nerby tries and fails to get free of Michael for a shot. He passes off, the shot is missed, and the Falcons race down the floor. This time Salt gets the shot fifteen feet from the basket along the baseline.

4–4.

The two teams trade baskets. 6–6, 8–8.

Suitcase scores on two straight offensive rebounds and a free throw. 10–8. 12–8. 13–8. Falcons.

Michael fouls Nerby on the dribble.

13–9. Falcons.

At half court Jack Armstrong takes a bullet pass from Suitcase that almost knocks him down. He recovers his footing and heads for the basket. Eighteen feet out, maybe too far out, he thinks, he stops and jumps. A defensive hand is right in his face. He has to pull the shot back a little and then release it with a high arch. The shot is good and he is fouled.

"If they play me that tight and still can't stop the shot," he thinks as he stands on the free-throw line, "they'll get frustrated."

He makes the free throw.

16–9. Falcons.

Hillsdale inbounds quickly and heads up the floor. The Hillsdale player with the soft, cradled shot scores twice from the very same spot that had opened the game.

16–11. 16–13. Falcons.

Seconds before the quarter ends I am already on my feet again. "Who the hell is that?" I say. Then I walk over to look at the scorebook. I run my finger down the Hillsdale lineup until I find it. Number forty-three. Rick Amend.

In elementary school he had always been too small for coaches to appreciate that he might have athletic promise. In basketball he sat on the bench more than he played, waiting to experience the same growth spurt that he watched his friends go through. But the spurt never came, and as a five-foot-two-inch freshman at Hillsdale, he remained as inconspicuous in athletics as he was small in real life.

But he was not discouraged by his size. He had been blessed with speed and quickness, and as a sophomore he went out for the Hillsdale jv football team as a running back. It seemed to be his fate again to sit on the bench, but halfway through the season his coach finally put him in a game. He was immediately breaking off long runs with defenders pursuing him like wolves chasing an antelope.

When he was a junior the varsity football coach tried to convince him to come out for the team. But as much as he loved football, and as much as it might have given him a chance to be a noteworthy scatback who for once did not sit unnoticed on the bench, he worried that taking his meager 125-pound frame onto a football field with 200-pound bruisers would get him killed. Instead, he wondered if he should go out for "C" basketball, where his size wouldn't matter but his speed would.

For days he agonized over what to do. When it became clear that the Knights' "C" team would be a good one, he chose basketball over the possibility of prominence in football. Besides, he liked Coach Wilkin, who was good-natured and so young that he stood out among teachers Amend thought of as "old codgers." He also liked Wilkin's willingness to play everybody, regardless of how good the opponent was or what was at stake. It meant that even if he wasn't a starter, he'd get to play.

When Wilkin saw Rick Amend's speed and defensive ability he made him a starter. For once he wasn't sitting on the bench, consigned to just watching the action. But even on the floor he remained an inconspicuous nobody who seldom scored and was a workhorse on defense. On offense he was perfectly happy to defer to the team's star, who everybody knew was Dan Nerby.

Hillsdale had started the season with five straight wins. A championship seemed more than just a possibility. Everybody wanted to win. Everybody played and nobody sat on the bench harboring the wish that they could play.

Meanwhile, the football team that Amend had thought about joining was horrible. "I made the right decision," he told himself.

The loss to Crestmoor the first round had been disappointing.

But Wilkin was still giving everybody a chance to play. And Rick Amend usually got the assignment to defend the opponent's most threatening player.

"Rick," Wilkin had told him before the Crestmoor game, "you've got Mike Thompson. He killed us last time. If we don't stop him, he'll kill us again."

Stopping Mike Thompson was a role that Amend relished. He knew he had the speed and determination to do it. Meanwhile, the idea that he would be Hillsdale's main offensive weapon was unthinkable. But on the first play of the game, when Dan Nerby hadn't been able to get a clear shot, he had passed off to Rick Amend on his left wing. As if it was his favorite move and he had performed it successfully again and again, Amend had driven up the middle, stopped, jumped, and scored.

Trotting back down the floor, he had told himself, "I'm gonna try that again."

At the break for the quarter, Billy Wilkin instructs his players and especially Dan Nerby, who is being smothered by Michael, to get the ball to Rick Amend. The first time Amend gets the ball in the second quarter, he takes what he thinks of as his "brand new shot," and it is good.

16–15. Falcons.

The Falcons, led by Michael, counterattack and score immediately

18–15. Falcons.

With Amend leading the Hillsdale scoring and both teams running the floor at breakneck speed, the two teams trade baskets. Every time the Knights pull within 1 point, Hillsdale fans shout and stomp the bleachers so hard that the whole gym shakes. They are certain they are about to take the lead. But each time the Knights score, the Falcons come right back and score within ten seconds.

The Falcons can't pull away and Rick Amend can't be stopped. He wrestles to get control of rebounds on Hillsdale's missed shots, then puts the ball in the basket. With each subsequent basket and as his confidence grows, he departs bit by bit from that first picture-perfect jump shot. He falls away or comes over the top of defenders, positioning the ball as he goes up. Halfway through the second quarter he pulls up from range and lets fly with a shot that seems taken in desperation. But the shot is good.

28–27. Falcons.

In football quarterbacks call it "being in the zone." It means that suddenly everything, including the linemen rushing at him, goes in slow motion. As soon as the quarterback releases the pass he knows it is a completion. In basketball it is called the "hot hand," and Rick Amend has it. On Amend's next jump shot he lands on the floor with his shooting arm still extended and his fingers flared, holding the perfect release of the ball. He watches the shot trace a high arc in the air and begins backpedaling to get back on defense. He knows as soon as the shot leaves his hand that it is good. It is precognition in its purist form. He doesn't suspect or hope or guess that the shot might be good. He knows with absolute certainty that it will be good.

For Amend it is the one night in a hundred when an otherwise inconspicuous figure on a basketball court suddenly finds himself in the shooting limelight. His body is invaded by some mysterious presence that is as commanding and spellbinding as hypnosis or speaking in tongues.

Amend scores twice more in the quarter.

36–31. Falcons.

36–33. Falcons.

With just seconds to go before halftime, Michael zigs and zags across the midcourt line on his way to the basket. Only Nerby is between him and 2 more points for the Falcons.

Michael swerves around Nerby, who is backing up as fast as he can. But it is not fast enough. Michael goes right by him and sees nobody ahead of him. He has, he thinks, a clear breakaway. He pumps one leg and soars for what he thinks is an easy layup. But as he extends his right arm, Nerby, whose body is crooked to avoid slamming into Michael, slaps the ball away

The ball bounces back toward the midcourt line. The Hillsdale players are already racing for their own basket. Nerby recovers the loose ball and races down the court. At the Knights' free-throw line, he passes to Amend, who receives the ball behind his own basket. Falcon defenders trap him along the baseline. In an effort to get out from behind the backboard, he jumps laterally and splits two defenders. He twists and contorts himself to somehow find a way to get the ball up toward the basket. His desperate move seems the logical consequence of attempts that have become more and more formless, in obedience to that hot-hand force that has taken over his body.

I jump to my feet and raise both hands, as if I also know the shot will be good and I am surrendering to scoring powers much stronger than I am.

But the ball smacks into the bottom edge of the backboard. 36–33. Falcons. Halftime.

FOURTEEN

The Gipper

I did not like inspirational, "win one for the Gipper" speeches. Whether they were delivered by nobodies or Knute Rockne, I found them of little use. Too often, I thought, halftime speeches that were meant to be inspirational ended up making otherwise loose players as tight as wood screws.

For me the urge to be brief and prosaic was a legacy of once having watched my father try to deliver an inspirational speech to his hapless but eager University of Minnesota Crookston Aggies. At halftime they were hopelessly behind and stood in a tight circle in a locker room that stank of analgesic balm. The ceiling of the locker room was hardly high enough for them to stand straight.

As his players waited for him to speak, there was nothing my father could say about tactics that would have made the slightest difference in the outcome of the game. So he chose to focus briefly on poise.

"Boys," he said, "I noticed when we fell behind," which was immediately, he didn't have to add, "some of you shuffled and hung your heads." He threw back his shoulders to demonstrate what he wanted. "I want you to stand straight," he said in a ringing voice. "Be proud. And don't bump your heads on the way out."

My halftime speech was as brief as my father's had once

been. "Amend is number forty-three," I said. "When we get back on the floor, all of you take a good, hard look at him. It's going to take all of you to stop him. So you've all got two men to stop. Your own man *and* Amend. Know where they both are at all times on the floor."

I noticed that Michael's jersey had flopped out from the breakneck speed at which he ran the floor. I paused in my halftime speech now to strike just the right brief, inspirational note, in the spirit of my father.

"Michael," I said, "tuck in your jersey."

All season long it has been first one Falcon and then another who has led the scoring. Michael, Jack Armstrong, the Professor, even Salt, whose role has been to rebound—they have all led the team. And it has been Suitcase who has carried them through the first half of the Hillsdale game.

"Whose turn is it now?" I wonder.

It is Jack Armstrong again. He scores four straight baskets in the third quarter, all of them variations of his float move. But in his efforts to help guard Amend, he picks up three quick fouls.

"Okay. Listen up," I say at the end of the third quarter. "We can't afford to have anybody foul out." I put three fingers in front of Jack Armstrong. "You've got three fouls. No more."

Periodically, the Knights have forgotten to cover the Professor deep. It has led to several sleeper baskets during the course of the game. "All of you, when we get possession, keep looking deep." For the Professor, I mean. "It's in mayhem like this," I say, referring to the deafening noise, "that little things can get lost." I pause, to see if any of my Falcon "little things" will smile at my play on words.

They don't.

"If the Knights forget to cover the Professor again," I finish, "get the ball to him."

I think I have said everything I need to say in the brief interlude between quarters. But then I look at the scoreboard. The Falcons are leading by 10 points. Again and again during the season the Falcons' scoring has exploded to create huge leads. The lead they have suddenly opened up has all the earmarks of another Falcon explosion.

But I shout now in an effort to be heard over the pep band music and the cheering. "This game is not over. They are too good to quit." I stop to catch my breath from shouting and I inhale the smell of hot popcorn and caramel apples drifting into the gym from the foyer. "It's Friday night in a pretty how town," I say, paraphrasing a line from the poet e. e. cummings, "and there's nothing else to do in quiet San Mateo but eat popcorn, watch a good basketball game, and cheer. These fans won't quit either."

The Knights explode in the fourth quarter. Despite the fact that every shot he takes is against two or three Falcons, Amend scores repeatedly and the Falcons' lead narrows.

54–46. Falcons.

54–48. Falcons.

There are no opportunities for full-court passes to the Professor. Every time the Falcons try to shoot, they are fouled. They miss one free throw after another. Michael misses three in a row and is back in the same frustrated frame of mind that haunted him earlier in the year.

After each missed free throw it is the Knights who come roaring back on the heels of the Falcons and continue to close the gap.

54–50. Falcons.

In a matter of minutes a 10-point lead for the Falcons has shrunk to just 4 points. The Knights are making "a run," physically and figuratively.

It is a unique feature of basketball that game polarities can be quickly reversed. A team that could do nothing right suddenly can do nothing wrong. Or a team that couldn't miss suddenly can't find the basket. Shots that snapped the net are air balls. Shots that swirled the rim and then went down the net like a corkscrew now fly out of the basket like cannonballs. Leads evaporate quickly.

With two minutes to go, it is Michael, not Jack Armstrong, who draws his fourth foul. I take a time-out and Michael heads for the Falcons' bench. As Michael passes the Hillsdale bench, Billy Wilkin steps away from his own team huddle and shakes Michael's hand. He thinks, mistakenly, that Michael has fouled out. "Nice job, son," he tells Michael.

Michael glances at him, his head tilted, confusion on his face that says, "Nice job for what? For missing three straight free throws?"

Michael trots on to the huddle in front of the Falcons' bench. The pep bands are on their feet, warlike combatants who are faced off on a battlefield but can hurl only artillery shells of noise at each other. In one of the pep bands, the bell of a huge tuba twists back and forth like a radar dish, following the beat of the bass drum. The cheering from the two opposing bleachers rolls into the middle of the gym like tidal waves that crash into each other and then throw spume into the air. Beneath it the deep rumble of feet pounding on the bleachers threatens to crack the gym in two right along the half-court line. It is either a coincidental but real California earthquake or something even worse, perhaps the earth delivering an apocalyptic swan song.

It is pointless for me to try to speak. Michael and the Whiz Kids all turn away from me and stare at the pandemonium in the bleachers.

Michael spots his mother and father for the first time. They are both standing. His mother's head is barely visible above the crowd, but she is waving at him. "I'm here!" her wave says. "I'm here!"

Jack Armstrong also spots his parents. It is the first game they have had an opportunity to see him play. He has never doubted their affection for him, but their presence in the bleachers now is an act of affection as powerful and emotional as an embrace.

The Professor looks for his father, who has cheered for him on baseball diamonds and time and again seen him in All-Star baseball games. But this is the biggest event of the Professor's athletic life and he scans the bleachers to see that his father is there, standing also, his face as reposed and satisfied as if he were playing Chopin instead of watching a thrilling basketball game.

Suitcase doesn't bother to look for his parents. He knows they aren't there. For them the noise and excitement of a basketball game means little or nothing compared to the drama of hair-raising escapes from Russians and Nazis.

Salt also can't find his parents, who have never seen him play in anything. "They didn't come," he tells himself.

The buzzer sounds. Michael and the Whiz Kids turn back to me. But I haven't said a word. So what was the time-out for?

I hold my hands out, palms up, to indicate the futility of trying to be heard above the mayhem.

They all nod. "Don't worry, Coach," they want me to understand. "Everything's under control. This is just what we like."

After the time-out the Falcons have no opportunity to run and they set up the Solar Eclipse play. Jack Armstrong has the ball alone on the point and he dribbles in place with the clock ticking down.

1:55 seconds.

He makes a few crossover dribbles in an attempt to get around his man but then backs up as if he has given up. He turns oblique to his defender to protect the ball and he passes to Michael, who has moved close to rescue him.

1:50 seconds.

Nerby jumps directly in front of Michael. This is exactly what Nerby wants. A chance to block the Falcons' leading scorer as he attempts to drive and shoot. Nerby is crouched, flicking his fingers, inviting Michael to try to get around him.

1:40 seconds.

After passing to Michael, Jack Armstrong cuts straight up the key, then curls off a double screen set by Salt and Suitcase, who are shoulder to shoulder with their arms crossed at the edge of the key.

Still with the ball, Michael takes one quick step to start his drive, then whips the pass midstep to Jack Armstrong as he curls off the screen, wide open. Fifteen feet from the basket he receives the pass and turns to jump and shoot.

56–50. Falcons.

The Knights inbound quickly and Amend scores immediately.

56–52. Falcons.

The Falcons miss, the Knights rebound and come flying down the floor again. It is a prelude to another run and Falcons fans are roaring, hoping that the noise will somehow hinder the Knights.

At midcourt, as if they have tried to dribble through the earthquake crack in the floor, the ball bounces loose and then flies between players. As soon as somebody seems to have it in his grasp it is batted loose again and the knot of players trying to get possession of it grows tighter and tighter, like a rugby scrum.

I stand up and try to shout a warning: whichever team comes out of the scrum with the ball will have a breakaway run to their basket.

It is the Professor who gets control of the loose ball and then streaks for his basket. The Knights are close on his heels,

Nerby coming the fastest. It could be a repeat of the out-of-the-blue block he made on Michael's shot earlier in the game.

In an effort to beat Nerby, who is closing fast, the Professor takes off early for a right side layup.

"Too early," I think.

But the Professor glides through the air, his tiny right hand cradling a ball that looks as big as a globe. When he lets the shot go, Nerby swats at it. But he is too late.

58–52. Falcons.

1:10 seconds.

The Knights counterattack and score.

58–54. Falcons. A 4-point difference again.

Suitcase steps out of bounds with the ball and looks deep for the Professor. But the Knights have him covered, so Suitcase hurls a sweeping hook pass to Jack Armstrong at midcourt. He heads down the right side, then does his crossover dribble and drives for the key.

Two retreating Knight players are already there, waiting for him. It is the perfect situation for his float move. He can take off on the run, split the defenders, then float until he reaches the basket.

The shot swirls on the rim as if the basket is a whirlpool that is about to suck the ball into the net. Then it flies out.

Crestmoor fans explode with a moan.

58–54 still. Falcons.

Knights' ball. 0:50 seconds. Here they come again. How many times can they mount a comeback? This will surely be the last time they can make a run. There just isn't enough time on the clock.

The Knights miss.

Suitcase gets the rebound but Nerby is immediately clawing at him in an effort to steal the ball. Suitcase manages to look deep and sees that the Knights have indeed forgotten "little things." The Professor is all alone and waving for the ball.

Suitcase throws a long, powerful pass. The ball travels at such speed that, if anything, it is rising in flight. Every head in the gym is swinging in unison to follow the flight of the ball. It is as if they are tennis fans following the back-and-forth action in a tennis rally.

The pass is high. The Professor has to jump and stretch to snag it. By the time he has the ball under control, the Knights are about to surround him.

He jumps quickly and scores.

60–54. Falcons.

0:35 seconds.

It is a "take that!" blow from the Falcons. The Knights can't possibly come back and score again. But they are like punch-drunk fighters who stagger and steady themselves and then come flying back down the floor.

The heads swivel again. This is basketball as it should be, back- and-forth action without tactical time-outs, fouls, or free throws that stop the game cold. This is the end of a game that has been a magnificent stage play, with the tension screw being wound tighter and tighter. It would be as much of an outrage for me or Billy Wilkin to stop it with a time-out as it would be for a director to leap onto the stage in the final gripping scenes of a play to give directions to the actors. The last seconds of this game represent the end of a melodrama in fast-forward. The actors on the basketball stage already know what to do. They have rehearsed it again and again. A time-out by either coach to prompt them with their lines would be superfluous. Besides, in the bedlam no one would be heard.

The Knights miss. The Falcons counterattack immediately. But Nerby steals the ball at half court, drives for the basket, pulls up at twenty feet, shoots, and misses.

Salt rebounds and finds Jack Armstrong at half court. He starts to his right, reverses to his left, then back right again.

At the free-throw line, he jumps. The shot snaps the net. He lands but doesn't put a fist in the air, pump one arm, or signal "V" for victory to the stands. His basket is all in a day's heroic work.

62–54. Falcons.

0:20 seconds.

The action has been so fast and furious that players are scattered all over the court. The Knights throw the same quick, deep pass that is the mark of the Falcons' ten-second offense. Michael flies in the air, picks off the pass, and before he lands he hurls the ball to the Professor.

Fifteen feet from the basket, his favorite deadeye spot, the Professor shoots.

64–54. Falcons.

0:10 seconds.

The Knights jerk the ball out of the net and all five of them race for their basket in an effort to score once more, even if it is hopeless and they have lost. But they can't just quit and walk off the stage before the curtain comes down. They have the last lines of the play.

"We didn't quit!" the script says.

They don't even stop when the buzzer sounds. It doesn't matter that time has run out. There is no clock with seconds ticking down that cuts short the will to win.

Falcon fans are rushing onto the court. Michael and the Whiz Kids are at the center of a tangle of bodies. They are arm-in-arm in a tight circle, just tiny figures leaping together into the air.

For five minutes after the game was over, none of the fans in the bleachers left but instead stood clapping. The applause was not just for the speed and nonstop energy of the victors. Nor was it simply homage paid to the losers, who had never led after the first minute of the game but had refused to give up. The applause was for *both* teams and the last two minutes of thrilling play, when the players had streaked up and down the floor like Roman candles.

Those spectators watched as the Falcons, led by Edward R. Murrow, tried to lift Michael on their shoulders so that he could cut down the net. But stacked two high the Falcons were still too short to reach the net. Somebody brought a stepladder. His mother and father watching, along with one of his uncles, Michael climbed the ladder and then discovered that he had no way to cut down the net.

It was Michael's uncle who shouted up to him, "You need a knife?"

As deferential as ever, Michael answered, yes, he needed a knife.

His uncle reached in his pocket and pulled out a switchblade. He opened the long blade with a sinister snap.

"Oh, god! Oh, no!" Michael thought.

But at that moment nobody paid attention to racial stereotypes. Michael slashed at the net and quickly had it draped around his neck, as if it were expensive jewelry instead of just string.

"We met our goal," Michael thought as he climbed down the stepladder.

But the thrill of it was offset by the realization that it was over. No more games of "twenty-one" at practice, with everybody laughing and whooping and dashing back and forth. No more racing up and down the floor. No more full-court maneuvering where he knew nobody could stop him. No more jump shots that were swallowed by the basket so cleanly that for an instant the net seemed to be fattening itself.

Heading for the locker room, Rick Amend felt one of the cheerleaders patting him on the back. He had been the game's leading scorer. Relying mostly on his newly discovered shot, he had tallied eleven field goals and the Falcons had not been able to stop the "inconspicuous nobody" who had had the night of his life.

Once inside the Knights' quiet locker room, Dan Nerby shook the hand of every one of his teammates. They had all played well, he told them. "Don't worry about defeat." Then Billy Wilkin told his players, "You are the best team I've ever coached. But the Falcons are the best lightweight team I've ever *seen*."

As good as the Falcons each were, they all credited someone else on the team as the source of their power:

Suitcase said they won because they always looked for the Professor.

The Professor pointed to Jack Armstrong as the team quarterback.

Jack Armstrong credited the championship to the rebounding of Salt.

Salt said Michael was so good he was intimidating.

Michael praised Suitcase's quiet determination.

In a postseason summary that he titled "Crestmoor Champions," Edward R. Murrow celebrated them all with journalistic hyperbole. Michael had so many moves fans never saw the same one twice. Jack Armstrong was "Mr. Inside and Mr. Outside." The Professor was the offensive "backbreaker." Suitcase shot so quickly that no opponent knew it was coming until it was too late. Salt leaped for rebounds as if he were shot from a trampoline.

In an effort to copy the tradition of Coach Red Auerbach of the Boston Celtics, who always lit and then puffed on a victory cigar on the bench, I also tried to light one in the locker room while Michael and the Whiz Kids watched and laughed. I began choking immediately and flushed the cigar down a toilet. It was one more case in point, if anybody needed it, that with my bizarre ten-second offense and my disavowal of Gipper speeches I was ill-equipped to follow the Protocols of the Elders of Coaching.

Edward R. Murrow, in his sport coat and ascot, celebrated the loudest in the locker room. The witty klutz whose jump shot was laughable pounded everybody on the back.

"You buried them," he told me.

"Buried them? That was the closest 10-point game in the history of basketball."

Newspaper headlines the next morning read, "Earthquake Shakes Fourteen Midwest States." The powerful quake had made skyscrapers in Chicago teeter. But nothing was as earthshaking or extraordinary as the news that a basketball game between two miniature teams in California had been so hard-fought in front of so many rabid fans that the floor had seemed to crack, and Michael and the Whiz Kids had emerged as champs.

FIFTEEN

Jimmy the Greek and Artichoke Joe

Saturday night after the victory over Hillsdale, Michael Thompson celebrated by dating the same girl in whose closet he had hid. He was a little less secretive about dating her now, but he remained reluctant to meet her family. "They would have been uncomfortable," he explained.

In the spring of 1969 the Professor decided to run for president of the student body. "I want you to be my vice president," he told Michael.

Michael lifted his head. "You've got to be kidding."

"You'll get a chance to talk, to start speaking more."

"That's just what I *don't* want to do."

Eventually he agreed to run, but he expected to lose, not because he was the only black student at Crestmoor and he thought nobody would vote for him, but because the idea of election speeches terrified him. What could he say about himself that wouldn't sound like bragging? What could he say about his childhood in Madill, or his early blindness, or even the Crestmoor championship that he and the Whiz Kids had won— what could he say about any of it that would make him electable?

In the school's Little Theater, packed with students, he delivered the first and only speech of his life. His feet sweating in his desert boots, he stood at the microphone while the audience waited in absolute silence.

"Hi," he said. "My name is Michael Thompson."

The audience immediately erupted into laughter at the idea that he felt the need to explain who he was.

When they stopped laughing he said simply, "Vote for me." Then he sat down.

He and the Professor won in a landslide. Afterward he joked, "The student body must be crazy."

His mother was ecstatic. "Michael Ralph," she said, "do you see what you can do when you put your mind to something?"

He did not bother to tell her that his mind was not into politics, at any level.

Later that spring Crestmoor's seniors gathered in a Peninsula bowling alley to hold their traditional Senior Night, a dusk-to-dawn celebration of their upcoming graduation. Michael was reluctant to go until the Professor convinced him that it would be a night for celebration and revelry. Michael and the Professor spent much of the night at a ping-pong table, defending themselves against all comers, none of whom could beat them. Then a hypnotist performed and put selected students in deep trances where they clucked and flapped their wings like chickens. When Michael's turn came he could not be coaxed into a trance in which he had no control over who he was.

Before the evening was over his classmates all lay on the floor and formed a boy-girl human chain that represented how close and connected they had become in just four years. Somewhere in the middle of the chain, connected to gorgeous classmates on either side, Michael told himself that he was no longer the isolated figure whose parents had braved racism and exclusion to settle in San Bruno.

On the June afternoon before graduation ceremonies in the Crestmoor gym, Michael wrenched his ankle playing basketball near his home in Rollingwood. He limped home, his ankle obviously broken, but he told his worried mother only, "I sprained my ankle." That night, unable to keep to the slow strides of the "Pomp and Circumstance" processional, he hobbled to the stage. A decade later there would be twenty-five black students enrolled at Crestmoor High. But Michael Thompson had been the first, blazing a trail through territory that was as strange to him at first as the Amazon. He hadn't done it with a machete or with gun bearers to protect him. He had done it quietly, alone, with his head down and little to say except, "Vote for me." When he limped across the stage to receive his diploma, the cheering lasted for a minute before the ceremony could continue.

That fall he entered Skyline College in San Bruno to play basketball and study sociology. Midyear he quit the college with the intention of marrying the neighborhood girl who was pregnant with his son. But her parents forbade the marriage and for the next twenty years, as his son grew up, Michael played basketball wherever the opportunity presented itself. Romances came and went. He began working as a mail-room clerk and eventually worked his way up to being a computer programmer in Silicon Valley, staring all day long at strings of programming code.

In 1983 Michael flew back to Madill to visit his birthplace. While he visited with one of his aunts, he was told by a relative that Jim Thompson was not his father.

He was stunned. Neither his mother nor his father had ever told him.

"I thought you knew," the relative said.

"I *didn't* know."

As soon as he was back in San Bruno he confronted his mother. "Is this true?"

Yes, she said, it was true. "Who told you?"

He explained that he had heard it as a whispered rumor while he was in Madill.

She told him never to bring it up again. His father was Jim Thompson, and that was that.

It had been his tiny mother who made sure he took advantage of each opportunity that presented itself in San Bruno. As she approached her seventies, she followed every hiccup and development of Michael's life as if he were still a teenager at Crestmoor High instead of in his forties. Then in 1995, still in the house on Catalpa, she suffered a massive stroke. As Michael watched from her bedside, ambulance medics tried to revive her. In a matter of hours she was dead.

She was the woman who had called him "Michael Ralph" when she wanted to remind him of the dignity of his life and to behave himself. "She may have been small," Michael thought, "but she was big in everything." Now she was gone. For weeks Michael went to work and sat staring numbly at the computer screen. He talked to no one. In the evenings he watched television for hours without the slightest interest in the programs. Even the game of basketball seemed pointless. The superb athlete who had once been able to fly up and down a basketball court all night long could hardly summon the energy to get up and go to bed.

In 2002 Jim Thompson also died in the home on Catalpa where Michael had grown up. It was then that Michael began to appreciate that he could never have had a better father than the one he acquired by default. Despite Jim Thompson's fancy hats, which Michael had copied out of respect, his quiet but steady life had been exactly what Michael had needed to be tethered to during the uncertainties he experienced in those first days in San Bruno. Without ever once lecturing or preaching, Jim Thompson had made it clear to Michael that being confined to a black neighborhood wasn't any more "separate but equal" than being locked in a classroom with only black classmates. San Bruno was where Michael could at least have an opportunity to improve himself.

San Bruno was where he could at least have an opportunity to develop ambition.

With both his mother and father gone Michael became even more despondent. He and his younger brothers sold the house on Catalpa and Michael bought a small camper. For six months he lived in the camper, parking on San Bruno streets or at shopping malls for one or two nights before moving on so the police wouldn't harass him. All the promise of his life as a student and basketball star at Crestmoor High seemed gone.

One night he returned to his camper to find it surrounded by police. While the police radios crackled with emergency calls for backup during a nearby robbery, they searched his van.

"There's a robbery going on," he said, "and you're messin' with *me?*"

One day not long after, trying to negotiate a tight turn in San Bruno, both eyes fogged up and he crashed into the curb. He abandoned the camper and walked home. Over the next five years he had numerous appointments with ophthalmologists at the San Mateo County Hospital to diagnose what was wrong. What was wrong was that the work of staring at a computer screen all day long had aggravated his vision. He needed to have eye surgery. There was no point in operating to restore the vision in his left eye. It was gone. But the doctors recommended immediate laser surgery to his right eye, to stop the deterioration. "It's a wonder you've haven't gone blind already," they told him.

After the surgery he took eye drops four times a day. Each day he had to lie down for an hour in a dark room and close his eyes. He couldn't drive. He could no longer work at a computer and he left his job. He filed for workers' compensation. They conceded that that his left eye was useless. "But your right eye is good," they said. "You can still do computer work."

In June 2010 it had been over forty years since Michael and the Whiz Kids had thrilled basketball fans on the Peninsula. Rival San Mateo High, too timeworn to withstand the earthquake that everybody said was coming, had been torn down. A huge grabber machine with jaws had taken brick bites out of the walls of the old school, gorging itself on history. It had been only a matter of weeks before the school was gone. Meanwhile, what was newest and without tradition in American society had also become vulnerable, and Crestmoor High was closed because of declining enrollment. They locked the doors and turned out the lights. Not long after pranksters drove a caterpillar through the gym wall. It left a hole so big it looked as if the gym had been hit by a cannonball.

For me the disappearance of the two schools was a reminder that nothing lasts and I began searching for Michael and the Whiz Kids before they also disappeared from history. One by one I found them. Jerry Barclay, the all-American boy who had lived the adventures of Jack Armstrong in a buckeye park in San Bruno, graduated with a degree in architecture from the University of California at Berkeley. David Wright, the Professor no bigger than a baseball cap, went to work in the timber industry and retired in Oregon. I found David "Salt" Saltenberger working in Reno and living with his wife in a secluded home in the California mountains. Arnis "Suitcase" Rapa lived with his wife and three children in Temecula, California, where he worked as a medical technician. David Esposto, for whom I could not find an appropriate nickname, graduated from Cal Poly San Luis Obispo and became an aeronautical engineer. Darrell Hirashima, the only one of the Whiz Kids to take up coaching basketball, died of a heart attack in 2008. But I found his family in the East Bay. Edward Sessler, who could have been another Edward R. Murrow, had become a tech writer in

Silicon Valley. He also had died not long into the new millennium.

None of the former Whiz Kids or their families could tell me where Michael Thompson was. He had simply disappeared. For months I searched for him. I found clippings from the school's student paper that made a brief reference to Michael having once played basketball for the Mormon Church. Surrounded by computers that glowed like square moons in a small, dark room of the Family History Center of the Mormon Church in San Bruno, I searched for any signs of the Thompson family. The church's genealogical records were legendary. Families from all over the world dug into them seeking ancestors and disappeared friends. I could find nothing. The archivists finally told me, "He must not have been a Mormon."

Then the Professor e-mailed me to tell him that he had found two addresses in San Bruno where members of the Thompson family were still living. One was the old address on Catalpa. On September 8, 2010, I drove the streets of San Bruno and Rollingwood looking for the house on Catalpa. When I finally found the house it was protected by a high fence from behind which came the menacing barking of a pit bull. The Hispanic girl who came to the fence gate could speak no English. But she made it clear that she and her parents had lived in the house for years. "Mi casa," she repeated over and over. "Mi casa." The next day the trunk gas pipeline on the very same streets I had driven exploded. I watched from the safety of my home as the holocaust unfolded on television and made national news. I had just missed being incinerated, which would have brought my search for Michael to a fiery end. "It is ordained that I find him," I told myself.

The second address the Professor had given me was a duplex on Easton Street in lower San Bruno. Half the houses on the street had grated windows and white rock lawns. The other half had wrecked cars in their narrow driveways.

I knocked on the door of the downstairs duplex with all its shades drawn. There was no answer. For three days I returned to the duplex and pounded on the door. On the fourth visit I spotted a teenager with a baseball hat poking beneath the lifted hood of a muscle car parked in the duplex driveway.

I introduced myself and explained my purpose. I pointed to the duplex with the shades drawn. "Who lives there?"

"Nobody. It's been abandoned for years."

"Who *used* to live there?"

"I don't know."

"Who would know?"

He tugged at the bill of his baseball cap. "I guess my mother would."

"Is she home?"

"She's upstairs, watching *Oprah.*"

I explained again what I was after. The teenager went upstairs to talk to his mother while I waited in the street.

In fifteen minutes the teenager came back to his muscle car. "Michael Thompson lived there and then moved out. His son also lived here, but that was a few years ago."

"Does your mother have any idea where Michael Thompson is today?"

"No."

"Would any of the neighbors know?"

"I don't think so. The last my mother heard he was homeless, pushing a shopping cart and sleeping in the park at the end of this street."

I glanced at the end of the street. "Nobody's seen him recently?"

"I don't think so."

It was another dead end, I thought. I thanked the teenager and was about to leave.

The teenager tugged at his cap bill again. "My mother says Michael Thompson's son works at a mattress store in South City."

My hopes suddenly lifted, I thanked the kid and left. The park at the end of the street was Forest Lane Park, a narrow strip of dead grass covered with the windblown bark of eucalyptus trees. There was a small cement basketball court at the foot of a freeway berm. One lonely fan-shaped basket grew out of the cracked cement like a huge weed. Despite the suggestion that Forest Lane Park was a bucolic setting, the freeway noises were deafening. It seemed an unlikely place for anybody to spend the night trying to sleep.

It took five minutes to find the nearby mattress store where Michael's son was supposed to work. The store manager, who wore a plastic nametag, called up a list of his employees on his computer.

"He's not here," the manager told me.

"Was he ever here?"

"No."

For two months I chased down other leads given to me by Michael's former Crestmoor classmates. All of them were dead ends. Finally I called a retired San Mateo police detective whom I had met while working on the story of the only unsolved triple homicide in California.

Did the detective know any private investigators, I asked, who were good at finding lost persons?

The retired detective explained that he knew a husband-and-wife team of private investigators who worked out of San Mateo.

Perfect, I thought. I called them immediately. I explained that I had been a teacher and coach at Crestmoor High and I was trying to find a former student. The wife, whose silence to that point had seemed discouraging, stopped me. "—You taught at Crestmoor?"

"Yes."

"My father taught there."

"What's your father's name?"

"Jim Cokas. Do you remember him?"

"Of course I remember him. 'Jimmy the Greek.' He was the athletic director when I was coaching."

Now the wife was enthusiastic. "Tell me again what you're after."

I again went through the story of my 1968 "C" basketball team and my search for Michael Thompson. When I was finished the woman told me, "That's a great story. We'll find him."

The first efforts of the private investigators were as fruitless as mine. A "curly-haired woman" who was supposed to be a former fiancée of Michael knew nothing. Several Peninsula homeless shelters had never heard of him. The addresses on Catalpa and Easton yielded nothing.

Finally Jimmy the Greek called me. "My daughter tells me you're looking for a former Crestmoor student."

"Michael Thompson. Do you remember him?"

"Sure, I remember him."

Jimmy the Greek explained that since leaving Crestmoor he had gotten a private detective's license so that he could put to use the investigative skills he had learned tracking down truant students. "If Michael's on the Peninsula, or anywhere in California for that matter, I'll find him."

Two weeks later he called me. "Meet me Saturday morning at the Salvation Army homeless kitchen in South City."

"Have you got anything promising?"

"They keep track of who takes their meals there. We can check it out."

The kitchen had no records of Michael Thompson but promised to ask around. Then Jimmy the Greek drove me to the St. Vincent de Paul homeless kitchen in a narrow alley off Grand Avenue in South City. The tight alley smelled of rotting lettuce. The benches in the alley were filled with hungry, unshaved, homeless men who looked dazed as they wolfed down lunches out of Styrofoam boxes. I shuddered at the idea that Michael Thompson could have sunk so low. But the staff serving lunch said they had no record of him, ever.

"Some dead ends," I thought, "are hopeful."

Two weeks later Jimmy the Greek called me. "Write this down," he said. "Michael Thompson's son is working part-time in a mattress store in South City."

It didn't sound promising. "I already *went* there," I said. "They have no record of the son working there."

"Which store did you go to?"

"Sleep Train."

"You went to the *wrong* mattress store. The son is working at Bedroom Xpress."

I drove immediately to the store. I made several perfunctory investigations of mattresses before a clerk approached me.

I got right to the point and explained who I was and my search for Michael. Apparently, Michael Thompson's son worked at the store, I said.

The clerk nodded. "Yes, he works here. He doesn't come in until tonight."

"Would you give him a message to pass along to his father?"

"Sure. The son is a responsible kid. Hardworking. I'll tell him to tell his father that his high school basketball coach is looking for him."

Two days later I was in my den with a view north to the San Francisco skyline and across the bay to Oakland. "He's out there someplace," I told myself. "One person among a million. A needle in the haystack."

Then the phone rang. "Coach," the voice said. "This is Michael Thompson."

I sit in a dark corner of Artichoke Joe's, the one-time saloon and card room that had expanded into an imposing gambling casino in San Bruno. It is this same dark corner of the saloon in which I and my teaching colleagues used to gather on Friday afternoons to drink beer, eat popcorn out of pie tins, and wind down after a week of teaching.

The wood floor of the bar is no longer covered with sawdust or popcorn. Otherwise, little has changed over forty years. The room is as dark as midnight. Mock gaslights and Tiffany lamps with huge globes hang from the ceiling like eerie planets in a black void. Barrels serve as bar stools. Bright neon beer signs—"Bud Light," "Miller Genuine," "Widmer's"—accentuate how murky the rest of the bar is. A weather-beaten wood sign, barely readable on the wall above the table where I sit, reads, "Sir Walter Raleigh smoking tobacco. Can't bite, smells sweet." The saloon is redolent with the smell of whiskey.

The door to Artichoke Joe's opens and a searchlight beam from the afternoon sun spills into the bar. A figure enters and stands for a moment in the light like a faceless shadow cutout.

I stand up. "—Michael?"

"Coach!"

We hug each other awkwardly, then sit down at the table where I have been waiting.

Michael wears a black watch cap. His face is full and he is no longer the tiny bag of bones of forty-two years ago. He is missing several lower teeth. His left eye drifts. But his head is up. As he explains to me where he has been the past four decades, his voice is strong and fast and clear. He talks about his computer work, his failed romances, his son, his trip back to Madill.

"I've been looking for you for months, Michael."

"I've been right here in San Bruno."

"I heard you were living on the streets."

He shakes his head. "Not really. After my folks both died, I fell off the deep end. It was months before I could start to take pride in myself again."

"What are you doing now?"

He explains that for the past two years he has been living and working in a shelter in San Bruno. In exchange for his room and board, he works as the sole caregiver for a middle-aged stroke patient. While he works at the shelter, he waits for the resolution of his workers' comp case. "My eyes won't let me get back into computer work. I filed a claim for workman's comp. But the state is broke. At first they denied my claim. Then I got an attorney to help me file an appeal. We're still waiting for them to respond. If I ever do get workman's comp, it won't be very much. But I don't need much. I don't see well enough to drive anymore. But I've got a bicycle. If I need groceries I ride my bike to the store."

"Do the shelter people treat you okay?" I ask.

Michael nods. "They treat me fine. When I first went to work there, one of the patients called me 'boy' and 'nigger.' The manager of the shelter threatened to throw him out. 'If you can't get along with Michael Thompson,' the manager told him, 'you gotta move.' The folks at the shelter think I've got a good story to tell, and they want me to go talk to a group of local fifth-graders. You know how I used to hate to talk? That's gone. I'll talk to those fifth-graders. They've got their whole lives ahead of them."

"Who told you I was looking for you?"

"My son. He told me, 'There's a guy looking for you.' I said, 'Who?' He said, 'All I know is he's a writer. He wants to write a book about you and the little guys you played basketball with at Crestmoor.'"

We order lunch, cheeseburgers and French fries. Michael talks about his boyhood in Madill and his first days in San

Bruno. *The two of us exchange memories of that 1968 "C"*
championship season. He recalls every detail of the fight
with the players from San Mateo. "I know why they were
so bitter. They thought they knew who I was. But how could
they know who I was? We'd never even talked."

The cheeseburgers come and Michael eats slowly. As I
watch, I am relieved to see that he is eating without the
hungry, dazed look of those homeless men I had seen.

"Michael," I say, "when they closed Crestmoor High in
1980, twenty-five black students received their diplomas.
But you were the first, over a decade earlier."

If he has any thoughts about what a brave pioneer he had
been, he doesn't express them. "Crestmoor taught me how
to get along with all kinds of people," he says. "It taught me
to sit back and listen." He pauses in between nibbling at his
French fries and glances at the TV screen in the corner, where
President Obama is giving a speech. "I wish my parents were
still living," he says, "to see we've got our first black
president."

He nibbles at another French fry and for a moment he
seems to disappear in his own thoughts about his family
being the first black family in San Bruno.

"I don't know how much longer I'll have my eyesight,"
he says finally. "I expect to be blind again." He pushes aside
the plate with his half-eaten cheeseburger. "I was lucky to
become a good basketball player. If I go blind now, I can be
thankful that at least I was able to see through those years
at Crestmoor. What I saw was all good. That's the only way
I can look at it. I don't want to get down. People are a lot
worse off than I am." He points at the brass-rail entrance to
the floor of the casino, where the card tables are packed with
gamblers. He smiles. "I'm happy with the hand I was dealt."

Sources

My sources, along with background reading and documentary sources, are organized below according to chapters. Within each chapter, I have organized the citations around specific subjects. My own recollections of events, often refreshed by my interviews with the Whiz Kids and others, are incorporated in each chapter.

1. The Whiz Kids

The Illinois Whiz Kids

"1941–42 Illini Ahead of Their Basketball Time," Illinihq.com, accessed October 16, 2010; "Clinton Post Office to Be Named for Gene Vance," fightingillini.com, accessed February 26, 2011; "1942–43 Illinois Fighting Illini Men's Basketball Team," *Wikipedia*, accessed February 26, 2011; "Vance a Living Legend," Illinihq.com, accessed February 26, 2011; "High School Area Change Slated," *San Bruno (CA) Herald*, February 11, 1965; "DeFelice Offers Hope for Crestmoor Athletics," *Crest* (Crestmoor High school paper), March 19, 1965.

Crestmoor Basketball History

Wingspread (Crestmoor High student yearbook), 1963–70; Judy Torkelson Babcock, "Crestmoor High Scrapbook," 1962–66; "Mills Varsity Downs Crestmoor," *Viking* (Mills

High student paper), January 17, 1969; "Crestmoor Close to Upset Win," *San Bruno Herald*, December 25, 1963; "Crestmoor C's and D's Move 4 More," *Crest*, October 29, 1963; "D Cagers Go 'Unwon' in Season MPL Play," *Crest*, October 29, 1965; Edward Sessler, "1968–69 Crestmoor Champions: Season Comments," unpublished manuscript, courtesy of Jerry Barclay; "Falcons Lose to Aragon," *Crest*, November 15, 1963.

Exponent System

John E. Spalding, e-mail messages to author, December 10, 12, 13, 14, 16, 2010; John E. Spalding, "Height Study," unpublished manuscript, courtesy of John E. Spalding; William Russell, *A History of the California Interscholastic Federation* (Wilson Printing, n.d.), 74–78; John Horgan, transcribed interview by author, November 1, 2010, San Mateo CA; "125's," 1978 *Galileo High School Yearbook*; "Interview: Vince Gomez," *Prelude* (San Francisco), December 1987, 23; Terry Christman, transcribed interview by author, October 25, 2010; Ron Berridge, transcribed interview by author, November 19, 2010, Belmont CA.

2. Michael

Michael Thompson, Doris and Jim Thompson

Michael Thompson, telephone interview by author, October 26, 2010; Michael Thompson, transcribed interviews by author, November 3, 10, 17, December 1, 2010, January 11, February 16, March 16, 2011, San Bruno CA; "Is Your Name Linda? Michael?" *Crest*, January 27, 1967; "Standard Certificate of Live Birth: Michael Ralph Gibbs," December 10, 1951, State of Oklahoma; "Amendment to Certificate of Birth: Michael Ralph Thompson," August 10, 2009, State of Oklahoma; "All League? Hardly Likely," *Advance-Star* (Burlingame CA), November 15, 1968; "Michael Thompson:

Medical Records, July 2005–May 2010," San Mateo County Medical Center, San Mateo CA.

Madill, Oklahoma

"Cold, Dry Wind" (weather in Madill OK), November 18, 1951, oldfarmersalmanac.com, accessed November 27, 2010; "Mystic Finds Body of Missing Farmer," *Daily Ardmoreite* (Ardmore OK), October 16, 1930; "1932 Shootout at the Corner Drug in Madill," youtube.com, accessed November 22, 2010; *Marshall County, Oklahoma* (Memphis TN: Books LLC, 2010), 6, 13; Margarette Redwine (Marshall County Historical and Genealogical Society, Madill, Oklahoma), telephone interview by author, November 17, 2010; Margarette Redwine, e-mail message to author, November 30, 2010; "Marshall County, Oklahoma," *Wikipedia*, accessed November 17, 2010; "Madill in 1910," okgen.web, accessed November 17, 2010.

Oil Mill Hill

Harrell Harris, "Black Communities," *Marshall County Oklahoma: Our Celebration of 100 Years* (Virginia Beach VA: Donning, 2007), 162–65; Earl Heath, "75 Years of Progress: Historical Sketch of the Southern Pacific," *Southern Pacific Bulletin* (1944).

San Bruno, California

Judy Torkelson Babcock, e-mail messages to author, July 27, August 10, 2010; Judy Torkelson Babcock and Jim Babcock, interview by author, August 24, 2010, Belmont CA; Dave Wright, transcribed telephone interviews by author, July 30, August 18, 2010; Barney Rinaldi, interview by author, October 26, 2010, Belmont CA; Barney Rinaldi, e-mail message to author, June 25, 2010; Jeff Bell, transcribed interviews by author, September 7, November 18, 2010, San Francisco; Jeff Boyle, e-mail messages to author, September 10, November 15, 2010; Terence Warfield, e-mail message to author,

December 14, 2010; Ron Etherton, e-mail message to author, September 10, 2010; Alan Lubke, e-mail message to author, September 5, 2010; Jean Belforte Todas, telephone interview by author, September 30, 2010; Darold Fredricks, *Images of America: San Bruno, California* (San Francisco: Arcadia, 2003), 26–28, 99, 104, 113, 121, 125–28; Kevin Sweeney, *Father Figures* (New York: Regan Books, 2003), 10, 79–80; Janet Parker Beck, *Too Good to Be True* (Far Hills NJ: New Horizon Press, 1991), 15, 17; Carl Nolte, "San Bruno Fire: A Neighborhood Changed Forever," *San Francisco Chronicle*, September 12, 2010; Darold Fredricks, "San Bruno People and Places," San Bruno History Association, n.d., 7–8, 12, 47–50, 60, 63, 80, 123; John Devincenzi, e-mail message to author, September 7, 2010; Billy Wilkin, transcribed interview by author, July 19, 2010, Belmont CA; Kevin Sweeney, transcribed interview by author, August 15, 2010, Piedmont CA; Pete Pontacq, telephone interview by author, October 7, 2010; Alan O'Brien, e-mail message to Judy Babcock, August 25, 2010; Dave Esposto, telephone interview by author, October 3, 1010; Mark Simon, transcribed interview by author, October 27, 2010, Redwood Shores CA; Alison Solina Unterreiner and Jean Grech Condé, transcribed interview by author, September 24, 2010, Belmont CA; Jean Grech Condé, e-mail message to author, September 27, 2010; Scott Callaway, transcribed interview by author, October 12, 2010, San Francisco; Wayne Harrison, e-mail message to author, September 7, 2010; "A Dream Still Deferred," *New York Times*, March 27, 2011; "Many U.S. Blacks Moving to South, Reversing Trend," *New York Times*, March 25, 2011; Larry Hernandez and Kathy Wilson, transcribed interview by author, July 31, 2010, San Francisco; Chris Williams, e-mail message to author, June 23, 2010; Chuck Cline, e-mail message to author, July 9, 2010.

3. Coach

Crestmoor High School History

"Congrats to Crestmoor," *Crest*, October 11, 1962; "They Said It Couldn't Be Done," "Sparks: Newsboy of the Year," *Crest*, November 21, 1962; Scott Callaway, e-mail message to author, January 20, 2011; Wayne Harrison, e-mail message to author, January 12, 2011; Judy Torkelson Babcock and Jim Babcock, interview by author, August 24, 2010, Belmont CA; Judy Torkelson Babcock, "Scrapbook: Crestmoor High, 1963–66"; Judy Torkelson Babcock, e-mail messages to author, July 27, August 25, October 12, 2010; "Grooming Indicates Conduct," *Crest*, February 21, 1963; "Parking Lot Pranksters," *Crest*, January 31, 1964; "Thoughts for Freshmen and Others," "C's, D's in Second Year," *Crest*, October 15, 1963; "Whose Little Sister Are We Anyway," *Crest*, May 29, 1963; "Court Gossip," *Crest*, June 11, 1963; "Sink or Swim," *Crest*, February 14, 1965; "Hail to Crestmoor in Wrong Key," *Crest*, March 20, 1964; "Discipline?," *Crest*, April 17, 1964; "Dispute Flames Up Over New Hands-Off Policy," "Crestmoor Student Enrollment at 931," *Crest*, September 25, 1964; "A Hairy Story," *Crest*, October 1, 1965; "Crestmoor's Dying Chivalry," "Tamerlane Throws Messages Off Bridge," *Crest*, November 20, 1964; "Justification for Federal Action in Civil Rights Movement," *Crest*, April 23, 1965; "Eight Schools Invade Crestmoor's Campus," *Crest*, May 21, 1965; "Wild Is the Wind," *Crest*, March 21, 1965; "Graduates' 'Firsts' Build New Traditions at Crestmoor," *Crest*, June 8, 1965; Terry Christman, telephone interview by author, October 25, 2010; Jim Hill, telephone interview by author, September 16, 2010; Michael Palmer, transcribed interview by author, October 7, 2010, Millbrae CA; Barney Rinaldi, interview by author, October 26, 2010, Belmont CA; "Coaches to Vote Tuesday," *Advance-Star*, September 1, 1968; "Dress Code: SMUHSD," *Advance-Star*, September 8, 1968;

"sm Teachers Form Union," *San Mateo Times*, October 9, 1968.

Crestmoor and the Haight-Ashbury
Dave Wright, transcribed telephone interviews by author, July 30, August 18, 2010; Jerry Barclay, transcribed interviews by author, July 6, 2010, San Francisco, August 13, 2010, Oakland; Kevin Sweeney, transcribed interview by author, August 15, 2010, Piedmont CA.

The King Assassination and Race Issues at Crestmoor
Ed Sessler, "The Death of Non-Violence," *Crest*, April 5, 1968; "Human Happening Here," "Crest Urges New Curriculum," "smuhsd Begins Human Rights Group," "Dialogue Begins," *Crest*, April 24, 1968; "chs Needs Black History to Understand Racial Strife," *Crest*, October 11, 1968; "Black History to Be Discussed Here," *San Mateo Times*, November 14, 1968; "School Minority Advisory Panel Named," *San Mateo Times*, November 15, 1968; "Crest Poll Results Interesting," "Black-White Youth Meet Here," "Comments from the Crest Poll on Racial Concern," "Sports Aid Negroes," *Crest*, May 10, 1968; Steve Gehre, Don Leydig, and John Devincenzi, transcribed interview by author, September 11, 2010, Truckee CA; Steve Gehre, transcribed interview by author, November 9, 2010, San Mateo CA; Laura Russo, e-mail message to Judy Babcock, August 23, 2010; George Robinson, transcribed interview by author, November 1, 2010, San Bruno CA; Ralph Daniels, transcribed interview by author, November 2, 2010, San Francisco; John Ward, transcribed interview by author, December 1, 2010, San Mateo CA; Sam Goldman, transcribed interview by author, July 2, 2010, San Francisco; Norm Smith, interview by author, October 19, 2010, San Francisco; Ron Etherton, interview by author, August 4, 2010, Encinitas CA; "Wild West Revisited," "Last of the Bad Guys," *Crest*, October 1, 1965.

Michael Thompson Lightweight Basketball History
"C-D Cagers Tip-Off Today," *Crest*, September 13, 1965; Michael Thompson, transcribed interviews by author, October 26, November 2, 10, 17, December 1, 2010, January 11, February 16, March 16, 2011, San Bruno CA.

Recruiting Michael Thompson, 1968
Dave Wright, transcribed telephone interviews by author, July 30, August 18, 2010; Michael Palmer, transcribed interview by author, October 7, 2010, Millbrae CA; Arnis Rapa, transcribed interview by author, November 27, 2010, Millbrae CA; Dave Saltenberger, transcribed interview by author, September 20, 2010, Truckee CA; Theresa Waskey Hirashima and Trish Hirashima, transcribed interview by author, July 1, 2010, Berkeley CA; David Esposto, telephone interview by author, December 3, 2010.

4. Suitcase and the Professor

Skaidrite Rapa
Arnis, Guntis, Gio, and Skaidrite Rapa, transcribed interview by author, December 26, 2010, Millbrae CA; Arnis Rapa and Guntis Rapa, transcribed interview by author, April 25, 2011, Millbrae CA; "Occupation of Latvia by Nazi Germany," "Latvia in World War II," *Wikipedia*, accessed November 28, 2010; "Operation Keelhaul," *Wikipedia*, accessed December 27, 2010; "Secret Files of Operation Keelhaul: The Story of Forced Repatriation," reprint from *Congressional Record*, 92nd Cong., 1st sess., September 24, 1970; "Danziger Werft," *Wikipedia*, January 20, 2011.

Arnis Rapa
Arnis Rapa, transcribed interview by author, November 27, 2010, Millbrae CA; Arnis Rapa and Guntis Rapa, transcribed interview by author, April 25, 2011, Millbrae CA; Guntis Rapa, e-mail message to author, January 18, 2011.

Dave Wright
Dave Wright, e-mail message to author, November 20, 2010; Jeanie Wright, e-mail messages to author, March 4, 9, 2011; Dave Wright, transcribed telephone interviews by author, July 30, 2010, August 18, 2010; Dave Wright, e-mail messages to author, July 25, 26, August 11, 18, November 17, 2010.

5. Jack Armstrong and Salt

Jerry Barclay
Jerry Barclay, transcribed interviews by author, July 6, 2010, San Francisco, August 13, 2010, Oakland; Jerry Barclay, e-mail messages to author, July 13, September 15, 2010, April 19, 2011; "Falcon 'C' Cager Averages 18 Points," *Advance-Star*, October 2, 1968; "Barclay, Four Other Falcons Top Scorers," *San Bruno Herald*, October 2, 1968; "Class Elections Underway," *Crest*, May 29, 1968.

Dave Saltenberger
Dave Saltenberger, transcribed interview by author, September 20, 2010, Truckee CA.

Nicknames
Sessler, "1968–69 Crestmoor Champions."

6. Zinji

Zinji and Lucy
"The 3 Million-Year-Old Man," July 10, 1994, newsweek. com, accessed September 26, 2010; Donald Johanson and Maitland Edey, *Lucy: The Beginning of Humankind* (New York: Simon and Schuster, 1981), 21, 274–75; Donald Johanson, *Lucy's Child* (New York: William Morrow, 1989), 167; "Hominidae," *Wikipedia*, accessed September 26, 2010.

History of Human Height
"Human Height," *Wikipedia*, accessed September 26, 2010;

"A Short History of Height," Macleans.com, accessed September 26, 2010; "Anthropometric History," *Wikipedia*, accessed September 26, 2010; Jared Diamond, "The Worst Mistake in the History of the Human Race," scribd.com, accessed September 26, 2010; "Human Height: History of Human Height," museumstuff.com, accessed September 6, 2010; "Height Comparison Over Last 150 Years in Some Countries," patientinfo/flash/grow-taller.com, accessed September 26, 2010; Glenn Elert, ed., "Height of an Adult Human," *Physics Facebook*, hypertextbook.com, accessed September 26, 2010; Stephen Jay Gould, *The Mismeasure of Man* (New York: W.W. Norton, 1981), 143–44; Stephen Jay Gould, *Dinosaurs in a Haystack* (New York: Crown Books, 1995), 137, 140; Jerry A. Coyne, *Why Evolution Is True* (New York: Penguin, 2009), 17, 200, 215; Harold E. Jones, "Approaches to the Study of the Individual," *American Journal of Sociology* 50, no. 4 (January 1945), jstor.org, accessed December 17, 2010.

Legendary Little Men
Dick Fregulia and Vince Gomez, transcribed interview by author, August 26, 2010, San Francisco; Seymour Smith, letters to author, April 8, November 11, 2010; "Willie 'Woo Woo' Wong, USF's little big man," SFgate.com, accessed October 25, 2010.

Bevo Francis and George Mikan
"A Team for the Ages," *Columbus (OH) Dispatch*, November 16, 2008; John Christgau, *Tricksters in the Madhouse* (Lincoln: University of Nebraska Press, 2004), 65–71.

California Exponent System
John E. Spalding, e-mail messages to author, December 10, 12, 13, 14, 16, 2010; "Morse Recalls First Basketball on Coast," *San Francisco Chronicle*, March 15, 1942; Gary Salzman, ed., *San Mateo High through the Years* (Berkeley CA: Lederer, Street

and Zeus, 1960); Spalding, "Height Study"; Russell, *History of the California Interscholastic Federation*, 74–78.

Lightweight Basketball in California
"Mission High Wins California Casaba Championship," *San Francisco Chronicle*, December 5, 1931; "Lowell's California Cage Team Has Long, Hard Schedule," *San Francisco Chronicle*, December 3, 1931; "Hapless C & D Hoopsters Seek First Season Win," *California Campanile* (Palo Alto High), October 19, 1956; "C & D Hoopsters Enter Final Stages of Season," *California Campanile*, November 2, 1956; "Vikes Oppose M-A," *California Campanile*, January 25, 1957; "Lightweight Basketball," 1952 *Galileo High School Yearbook* (San Francisco); "Three California Cage Battles Won," *San Francisco Chronicle*," November 7, 1931; John Horgan, transcribed interview by author, November 1, 2010, San Mateo CA; "125's," 1978 *Galileo High School Yearbook*; "Interview: Vince Gomez," *Prelude*, December 1987, 23; Terry Christman, telephone interview by author, October 25, 2010; Ron Berridge, transcribed interview by author, November 19, 2010, Belmont CA.

Edward Sessler
"Amazing Nose Knows It's Breathtaking," *Crest*, February 28, 1967; Sessler, "1968–69 Crestmoor Champions"; Sam Goldman, transcribed interview by author, July 2, 2010, San Francisco; Sam Goldman, e-mail message to author, July 12, 2010; Edward Sessler, "Splinters from the Bench," *Crest*, September 29, November 17, December 8, 1967, January 12, 1968; "Sessler, Simon, Tonge Head Spring Term Crest Staff," *Crest*, February 16, 1968; "Falcons' Top Fan," *Advance-Star*, October 4, 1968; John Devincenzi, transcribed interview by author, September 11, 2010, Truckee CA; "Teachers of Ed Sessler," memorandum to author from Rose Boché, November 16, 1967.

7. Rene and Firp

Crestmoor versus South San Francisco
"Harriers, Cagers Open," *Advance-Star*, September 20, 1968.

Rene Herrerias
Rene Herrerias, transcribed interview by author, January 11, 2011, Walnut Creek CA; cover picture, *Sport*, January 1950.

Crestmoor versus El Camino
"Crestmoor 66, El Camino 24," *San Bruno Herald*, September 20, 1968.

Crestmoor versus Capuchino
"Class C, D Teams Set at Cap Hi," *San Bruno Herald*, September 5, 1968; "Falcon Five Starts Title Drive," *Advance-Star*, September 22, 1968; "All League Falcon Five Wins Opener," *Advance-Star*, September 14, 1968; "Falcons Top Cap Cagers on Courts," *San Bruno Herald*, September 26, 1968.

Frank Firpo
Frank Firpo, transcribed interview by author, July 27, 2010, San Bruno CA.

Crestmoor versus Mills
"Falcon Cagers Roll on to 4th," *San Bruno Herald*, September 27, 1968; "Barclay, Four Other Falcons Top Scorers," *San Bruno Herald*, October 2, 1968; "Knights Still Unbeaten," *Advance-Star*, October 4, 1968; "Thompson vs Barclay," *Crest*, October 11, 1968.

Darrell Hirashima
Theresa and Trish Hirashima, transcribed interview by author, July 1, 2010, Berkeley CA; "St. Ignatius v. Miramonte Basketball Game," CD, courtesy of Trish Hirashima; Theresa Hirashima, e-mail messages to author, June 21, July 8, 2010;

"Hirashima Shows the Way," *Crest*, January 16, 1969; Terry Warfield, telephone interview by author, July 13, 2010; Trish Hirashima, e-mail messages to author, June 20, July 8, 2010.

8. Bob and Red

Burlingame High School
John Devincenzi, e-mail message to author, January 31, 2011.

Bob Milano
Bob Milano, transcribed interview by author, July 29, 2010, Walnut Creek CA; Bob Milano, e-mail message to author, August 27, 2010.

Frank Bettendorf
Frank Bettendorf, telephone interview by author, August 17, 2010.

Crestmoor versus Burlingame
"Falcon Five Edges Panthers," *Advance-Star*, October 4, 1968; Jerry Barclay, transcribed interview by author, July 6, 2010, San Francisco; Jerry Barclay, e-mail message to author, June 21, 2010.

Haight-Ashbury
Kathy Wilson and Larry Hernandez, transcribed interview by author, July 31, 2010, San Francisco; Mike Palmer, transcribed interview by author, October 7, 2010, Millbrae CA; Dave Wright, transcribed telephone interview by author, July 30, 2010; Jerry Barclay, transcribed interview by author, July 6, 2010, San Francisco; Dave Saltenberger, transcribed interview by author, September 20, 2010, Truckee CA; Tom Wolf, *The Electric Kool-Aid Acid Test* (New York: Farrar, Straus and Giroux, 1968), 6, 10, 34, 65, 256, 352–53, 379; Seth Rosenfeld, "Reagan, Hoover and UC Red Scare," *San Francisco Chronicle*, June 9, 2002; "4 Jailed in Dope Arrests," *San Bruno Herald*, February 11, 1965.

Greg Shaw
"Step into My Parlor," *Crest*, October 22, 1965; *Mojo Navigator Rock & Roll News*, October 5, December 22, 1966, April 1967.

9. Noah

San Mateo High History
Salzman, *San Mateo High through the Years.*

Noah Williams and African American History in San Mateo

Randy Williams, transcribed interview by author, October 18, 2010, San Mateo CA; "Leslie Alan Williams," smlibrary-foundation.org, accessed October 19, 2010; "Noted African-Americans in Early County History," *Daily Journal* (San Mateo), February 9, 2004; "Blacks Claim Harassment by Observers," *San Mateo Times*, October 4, 1968; "Student Walkout Dwindles," *San Mateo Times*, October 7, 1968; "A New Look at How Black Culture Grew," *San Mateo Times*, October 10, 1968; "Guidelines Are Set for Minorities Panel," *San Mateo Times*, October 11, 1968; "S.M. Black Pupils, Faculty in Meeting," *San Mateo Times*, October 11, 1968; "Prexie Tells Students," *San Mateo Times*, October 16, 1968; Norm Bostock, telephone interview by author, November 17, 2010; "Backers Chant 'White Power,' Charge a Political Frame-Up," *Advance-Star*, February 19, 1969; "Blacks Need Action, Not Dialogue," *Advance-Star*, February 21, 1969; "Destroy the Premise of White Supremacy," *Advance-Star*, February 26, 1969; Buz Williams, transcribed interview by author, November 4, 2010, Foster City CA; "CSM's Black Queen Abdicates in Protest," *Advance-Star*, November 3, 1968; Charles Douglas, transcribed interview by author, August 23, 2010, Foster City CA; Sam Johnson, transcribed interview by author, December 7, 2010, Foster City CA; Alonzo Emery, transcribed interview by author,

September 13, 2010, Foster City CA; Alonzo Emery, e-mail message to author, October 13, 2010; Larry Miller, transcribed interview by author, November 23, 2010, Aptos CA; "Tribble's Black History Course Stimulates Interest, Response," *San Mateo Hi* (San Mateo High student newspaper), October 1969.

San Mateo High and the King Assassination
"Trouble Begins after School Is Dismissed," "Student Riot Quelled," *San Mateo Times*, April 5, 1968; "Students March for 'Death of a Friend,'" *San Mateo Times*, April 6, 1968; "Reason for Violence, Tension at the School?" *Advance-Star*, April 18, 1969; "A Black View of the Incident," *Advance-Star*, April 20, 1969; "Meeting Seeks End of Discord at S.M. High," *San Mateo Times*, April 18, 1969; "High School Integration Plan," *Advance-Star*, November 17, 1968; Jim Snider, transcribed interviews by author, July 8, October 20, 2010, San Carlos CA; "Dialogue," San Mateo Union High School District, April 25, 1969; "San Mateo High's Reform Program," *San Francisco Chronicle*, April 24, 1969; Gus Hassapakis, transcribed interview by author, October 21, 2010, Belmont CA; Barry Miller, transcribed interview by author, September 27, 2010, San Carlos CA.

San Mateo High Basketball
"Community Gymnasium Opening at San Mateo High," *Daily Journal*, December 5, 2002; Jim Snider, "1968, 1969 C Season," unpublished summary; "Champion D's Ease to Title to Preserve Dynasty," "C, D Cagers Dynasty in Peril as Bearcats Tangle with Falcons," *San Mateo Hi*, October 1969; "Talented Hollis Sparks D's as Bearcats Roll on Undefeated," *San Mateo Hi*, November 1968; "Undefeated D's Top League; C's Finish in Third Place," 1969 *Elm* (San Mateo High student yearbook); Lavelle Ferguson, transcribed interview by author, August 19, 2010, San Mateo CA; Darnell Ferguson,

transcribed interview by author, August 25, 2010, San Carlos CA; *Elm*, 1966–69; "King Center Now Named Officially," *San Mateo Times*, September 17, 1968.

Crestmoor versus San Mateo at San Mateo
"Cage Team Rolls On," *San Bruno Herald*, October 10, 1968; "Shot Chart," Crestmoor v. San Mateo, October 8, 1968, courtesy of Jerry Barclay; Michael Thompson, transcribed interviews by author, November 17, December 1, 2010, San Bruno CA; Jim Snider, transcribed interview by author, July 8, 2010, Belmont CA.

10. Darnell

Billy Wilkin
Billy Wilkin, transcribed interview by author, July 19, 2010, Belmont CA.

Crestmoor versus Hillsdale
Bob Templin, "Hillsdale High School through the Years," unpublished manuscript; 1968 *Hillsdale Shield* (student yearbook); "Thompson vs Barclay," *Crest*, October 10, 1968; "Falcons Hand Knights First Cage Loss," *Advance-Star*, October 13, 1968; "Defense Chart," Crestmoor v. Hillsdale, October 10, 1968, courtesy of Jerry Barclay; "Pair of Sophs Lead Falcons to 8th Win," *Advance-Star*, October 20, 1968; "Cagers Earn Split with Classy Crestmoor," *San Bruno Herald*, October 17, 1968; "Falcon Five Wins 7th," *San Bruno Herald*, October 18, 1968.

The Teenie Weenies
William Donahey, *Down the River with the Teenie Weenies* (New York: Rand McNally Junior Editor, 1921), 1–4, 10, 17, 31, 43, 57, 60.

Crestmoor versus Cap, Mills, Aragon, Burlingame
"Thompson Takes MPL Score Lead," *Advance-Star*, October

30, 1968; "Crest Twenties Eye Cage Title," *San Bruno Herald*, October 24, 1968; "Falcon's First Cage Crown," *Advance-Star*, October 24, 1968; "Falcons Win 9th but Knights Still Alive," *San Bruno Herald*, October 25, 1968; "Birds Wing School's Third Athletic Title," *San Bruno Herald*, October 31, 1968; "CHS C Basketballers Eye Championship," *Crest*, September 27, 1968.

Darnell Ferguson
Darnell Ferguson, transcribed interview by author, August 25, 2010, San Carlos CA.

Crestmoor versus San Mateo at Crestmoor
"Basketball Prep for SM," *Advance-Star*, November 1, 1968; Jim Snider, transcribed interview by author, July 8, 2010, Belmont CA; Michael Thompson, transcribed interviews by author, November 3, 10, 17, December 1, 2010, January 11, February 16, March 16, 2011, San Bruno CA; Dave Wright, transcribed telephone interview by author, July 30, 2010; Dave Wright, e-mail message to author, November 17, 2010; Jerry Barclay, transcribed interviews by author, July 6, 2010, San Francisco, August 13, 2010, Oakland; Arnis Rapa, transcribed interview by author, November 27, 2010, Millbrae CA; Dave Saltenberger, transcribed interview by author, September 20, 2010, Truckee CA; "Crestmoor v. San Mateo," 8mm film, October 31, 1968, courtesy of Jerry Barclay.

David Esposto
David Esposto, telephone interview by author, October 2, 2010.

11. Uncle Tom

The Fight
Jim Snider, transcribed interview by author, July 8, 2010, Belmont CA; Darnell Ferguson, transcribed interview by

author, August 25, 2010, San Carlos CA; Michael Thompson, transcribed interviews by author, November 3, 10, 17, December 1, 2010, January 11, February 16, March 16, 2011, San Bruno CA; Dave Wright, transcribed telephone interview by author, July 30, 2010; Dave Wright, e-mail message to author, November 17, 2010; Jerry Barclay, transcribed interviews by author, July 6, 2010, San Francisco, August 13, 2010, Oakland; Arnis Rapa, transcribed interview by author, November 27, 2010, Millbrae CA; Dave Saltenberger, transcribed interview by author, September 20, 2010, Truckee CA; Michael Palmer, transcribed interview by author, October 7, 2010, Millbrae CA; Ralph Daniels, transcribed interview by author, November 2, 1010, San Francisco; Barney Rinaldi, interview by author, October 26, 2010, Belmont, California; "San Mateo 56, Crestmoor 53," *Advance-Star*, November 3, 1968; "Bearcats Upset Crestmoor's Championship Cage Team," *San Bruno Herald*, November 7, 1968; "Crestmoor v. San Mateo," 8mm film.

Bobo Groves
Capt. Renaldo "Bobo" Groves, letter to author, November 4, 1968.

12. Nerb

Will Slocum
Will Slocum, "The Incredible Candidate Scrapbook and Other Stuff, 1967–68," *Will Slocum Library* (Millbrae CA: Odbal Book, 1969); "How San Mateo County Voters Cast Ballots," *San Mateo Times*, November 6, 1968.

Hillsdale High School History
"Dress Code Invades Hillsdale High School," "Black History Offered," "Good Season for Mini Cagers," *Hillsdale Scroll* (Hillsdale High School student newspaper), September 26, 1968, courtesy of Bob Templin; "Teachers' Workshop Probes

Problems of Racist Society," *Hillsdale Scroll*, March 20, 1969; Tom Brignand, interview by author, May 10, 2010, Belmont CA.

Dan Nerby

Tim Nerby, transcribed interview by author, January 20, 2011, Redwood City CA; Billy Wilkin, transcribed interview by author, July 19, 2010, Belmont CA; Dave Esposto, e-mail message to author, October 4, 2010; Billy Wilkin, e-mail message to author, August 16, 2010.

Crestmoor versus Hillsdale at Hillsdale, Pre-Game

"Not a Drop," *Advance-Star*, November 8, 1968; 1969 *Hillsdale Shield*; "Basketballers Play Title Game Tonight," *Crest*, November 8, 1968; "Mini Cagers Aim for Dual Titles," *Hillsdale Scroll*, October 18, 1968; "'C' Hoop Crown on Line Tonight," *Advance-Star*, November 8, 1968; "The Standings," *Advance-Star*, November 3, 1968; "Two Bearcat Cagers Top MPL Scorers," *Advance-Star*, November 6, 1968.

13. Rick

Rick Amend

Rick Amend, transcribed telephone interview by author, January 29, 2011; Rick Amend, e-mail message to author, February 19, 2011.

Crestmoor versus Hillsdale, First Half

"Scorebook with Running Score," Crestmoor v. Hillsdale, November 8, 1968, courtesy of Jerry Barclay; Billy Wilkin, transcribed interview by author, July 19, 2010, Belmont CA; Dave Esposto, e-mail message to author, October 4, 2010; Billy Wilkin, e-mail message to author, August 16, 2010; Michael Thompson, transcribed interviews by author, November 3, 10, 17, December 1, 2010, January 11, February 16, March 16, 2011, San Bruno CA; Dave Wright, transcribed telephone interview by author, July 30, 2010; Dave Wright, e-mail message to author, November 17, 2010; Jerry Barclay, transcribed interviews by author, July 6, 2010, San Francisco, August 13, 2010, Oakland; Arnis Rapa, transcribed interview by author, November 27, 2010, Millbrae CA; Dave Saltenberger, transcribed interview by author, September 20, 2010, Truckee CA.

14. The Gipper

Crestmoor versus Hillsdale, Second Half
"Christgau's Cage Crew Takes Title," *San Mateo Times*, November 10, 1968; Michael Thompson, transcribed interviews by author, November 3, 10, 17, December 1, 2010, January 11, February 16, March 16, 2011, San Bruno CA; Dave Wright, transcribed telephone interview by author, July 30, 2010; Dave Wright, e-mail message to author, November 17, 2010; Jerry Barclay, transcribed interviews by author, July 6, San Francisco, August 13, 2010, Oakland; Arnis Rapa, transcribed interviews by author, November 27, 2010, April 25, 2011, Millbrae CA; Dave Saltenberger, transcribed interview by author, September 20, 2010, Truckee CA; "Nightlife the Good Life for Crestmoor Twenties," *San Bruno Herald*, November 15, 1968; "Falcon C's Win It, 64–54," *Advance-Star*, November 10, 1968; "Grand Slam for Falcon Twenties," *San Bruno Herald*, November 28, 1968; "Individual Statistics: Crestmoor C Team, 1968–1969," courtesy of Jerry Barclay; "Earthquake Shakes 14 Midwest States," *San Mateo Times*, November 9, 1968.

15. Jimmy the Greek and Artichoke Joe

Michael Thompson, Postgame
Michael Thompson, transcribed interviews by author, November 3, 10, 17, December 1, 2010, January 11, February

16, March 16, 2011, San Bruno CA; "Dave Wright, Mike Thompson," *Crest*, January 16, 1969; Judy Babcock, e-mail message to author, July 25, 2010; Dave Wright, transcribed telephone interview by author, July 30, 2010; Dave Wright, e-mail message to author, November 17, 2010.

End of Crestmoor High, Destruction of San Mateo High
Mike Bower, interview by author, December 16, 2010, San Mateo CA; "Crestmoor School Debate not Over," sfexaminer.com, November 24, 2010, accessed November 30, 2010; John Devincenzi, e-mail message to author, December 3, 2010.

Postludes
"Jerry Barclay," linkedin.com, accessed June 15, 2010; Dave Wright, e-mail messages to author, March 17, 18, 2011; "Darrell Hirashima: 5/01/1952–12/19/2008," orindamagic. org, accessed June 17, 2010; "Darrell: A Celebration of Life," program from Darrell Hirashima memorial service, January 25, 2009, courtesy of Theresa Hirashima; "Californian Parents Be Too Involved," sfgate.com, accessed July 8, 2010; "Hirashima Rises from Ash Once More," maxpreps.com, accessed July 8, 2010; "Edward Alan Sessler," memorial program, April 13, 2007, Saratoga CA; Sam Goldman, letter to author, April 16, 2007.

Searching for Michael
"NTSB Issues Update on the Continuing Investigation of the Natural Gas Pipeline Rupture in San Bruno, California on September 9, 2010," sanbruno.California.gov, accessed December 14, 2010; Dan Swanson, interview by author, September 4, 2010, San Bruno CA; Pete Bahnmueller, e-mail message to author, September 24, 2010; Debbie Cody (Cody Investigative Group, Burlingame CA), e-mail messages to author, September 24, October 11, 2010; Jim Cokas, e-mail messages to author, September 26, October 11, 19, 23, 2010;

Jim Cokas, telephone conversations with author, October 26, 2010; Lt. Anthony Barnes (South San Francisco Salvation Army), interview by author, October 23, 2010; Tony Barnes, e-mail message to author, October 23, 2010; Jim Cokas, telephone interviews by author, October 23, 26, 2010; Michael Thompson, telephone interview by author, October 26, 2010; Michael Thompson, transcribed interview by author, November 3, 2010, San Bruno CA.